"It's so relaxing that before you know it from your chin and head out into the big bad world; a non-nail biter. And I left there believing just that – never again would I nibble my nails… So did it work?... Every time I'm a little stressed and feel my hands making their way up to my face, I subconsciously bring them back down before I've even noticed what's going on. And that must be because of the hypnotherapy."
– Anna Lewis, Cosmopolitan

"We decided what we wanted to discuss, told Aaron what these areas were and he tried to reinforce our ability to overcome problems of anger or sadness while we were in a trance. In the week between our first and second sessions, it did seem to me that Ann and I were more solicitous of each other and more affectionate than usual – bordering on downright soppy
– over the weekend." – Nick Curtis, The Daily Mail

"Being hypnotised is, frankly, a bit weird. But not at all unpleasant. It's easy because you don't have to do any work (unlike meditation). Aaron does it all for you; you just have to follow his lead… So did it work? Well, four weeks later, I'm not entirely sugar free, but I've most definitely cut down. The best result is that I don't think about it as much, especially in those crisis moments."
– Lucy, Women's Health

"As I sat on the bus back from the appointment I felt like I'd had a nice nap, was refreshed and pretty content. However, one question was on my mind: When I reach home – with not just a packet, but a whole cupboard full of crisps at my disposal – will I cave in?... Well, it's day 14 and I've not – yet – eaten a single packet of crisps."
– Poppy Bilderbeck, Unilad

"Following a recommendation from my addiction counsellor I received two hypnotherapy sessions from Aaron in 2010 to help bring an end to my 20-year gambling addiction. I am delighted

to report that it is now 2024 and I haven't gambled since. With 14 years of abstinence without the slightest desire or inclination to gamble, I think it's fair to say that, for me at least, it definitely works. To anyone thinking of giving it a go, I hope it helps you too."
– Sandeep Karia, City Hypnosis client

"I wanted to say a massive thank you to Aaron for his help. I had four sessions earlier this year (2023) online. He completely changed my mindset and I finally feel like myself again after one year of disordered eating. It has been several months since my treatment and I feel like he changed my life!"
– Victoria Davidoff, City Hypnosis client

"I thought I would wait a while until I reviewed my experience. I went to see Aaron Surtees a year ago to stop me smoking. I'm happy to say I haven't touched a cigarette from the day I walked out of his office. Amazing considering it was one session! Thank you very much. I can't recommend you enough."
– George Woodward, City Hypnosis client

"I contacted Aaron because I needed help with eliminating emotions in my trading. Since I was in Miami, we did online video sessions and after the second session, I noticed a drastic change in my performance. I was finally able to enjoy the process of trading! He listened to all my sticking points and we've been fixing them one by one. He has also helped me fix my eating habits and emotional management. I'm eternally grateful to Aaron for his help and mentorship in drastically improving my mindset!"
– Alecxander Castro, City Hypnosis client

"After 57 years of smoking and my latest severe chest infection I decided to try Hypnosis. I had no idea what to expect, but I went with a positive attitude. I felt I was in good hands with Aaron as he had a calm and reassuring manner. By the time I got home I felt I never wanted another or felt the need for another cigarette. My doctor, wife and son are delighted! It has completely changed my life."
– Ted Stratford, City Hypnosis client

Subconsciously

Powerful Stories of Lives Changed
through Hypnotherapy
(and How You Can Do the Same)

Subconsciously

Powerful Stories of Lives Changed
through Hypnotherapy
(and How You Can Do the Same)

By
AARON SURTEES

ISBN: 9798302641625

Imprint: Independently published

Copyright 2024, Aaron Surtees

All views expressed in this book are those of the author and are not intended for use as a definitive guide. This work is owned in full by the primary author, Aaron Surtees. No part of this publication may be reproduced or transmitted in any form whatsoever without the written permission of Aaron Surtees: aaron@subconsciously.com

This book was produced in collaboration with ClioBooks.ai and Write Business Results Limited. For more information on their business book and marketing services, please visit: https://cliobooks.ai/ or contact the team via admin@cliotech.ai www.writebusinessresults.com or contact the team via info@writebusinessresults.com.

Acknowledgements

Thanks to my partner Dayra for supporting and encouraging me in writing my first book.

Please note none of the case studies featured in this book reveal the individual's correct names. I have also changed gender in a number of studies, and changed certain factual details to further protect each person's anonymity and privacy, which I hold very dear. However, the actual conditions and issues I dealt with are all accurate and help showcase the power of mindset shift through hypnotherapy.

Dedication

To all of my clients past and present, without you I wouldn't have enjoyed such a rewarding and eye-opening career. Thank you for putting your trust in me and for believing.

Contents

Acknowledgements   I

Dedication   III

Contents   V

Foreword   VII

Prologue   XI

Introduction   1

Part One: Building a Foundation for Happiness   7

Chapter One
Understanding Mental Blockages and Fear of Failure   9

Chapter Two
Transforming Negative Thoughts into Positive Expectations   27

Chapter Three
Letting Go of the Past and Being Present   42

Part Two: Regaining Control and Breaking Bad Cycles   57

Chapter Four
Overcoming Self-Confidence Issues   59

Chapter Five
Breaking the Cycle of Addiction and Bad Habits   75

Chapter Six
Stopping Procrastination   91

Part Three: Creating Lasting Change   113

Chapter Seven
Balancing Work, Aspirations and Family Life   115

Chapter Eight
Adapting to Modern Challenges and Embracing Change   137

Chapter Nine
The Transformative Power of Hypnotherapy   161

Conclusion   185

Did You Know?   189

About the Author   195

Foreword by Cherry Healey

Before I had hypnotherapy myself, I'd seen its transformative power through working on a BBC TV programme with Aaron. During filming, he worked with us to help people overcome their challenges and I was amazed by the results he achieved.

Fast forward several years and I was invited to be on *Celebrity SAS: Who Dares Wins*. Having been a fan of the show for years, I knew the level of challenges I was going to face, both physical and mental, and I knew that I'd need some help to get through everything they were going to throw at us. I have a fear of heights, and am also claustrophobic, both fears I would likely have to face during the show.

Just before I travelled to New Zealand for filming, I contacted Aaron for a hypnotherapy session. We did our session via video, during which time Aaron used hypnotic suggestion around "You are fearless, you can cope under any level of pressure and stress", "You have no fear of heights, you feel in complete control of anxiety at height", and "You feel able to effortlessly control anxiety".

Aaron also included some affirmations and visualisations in our session. When I travelled to New Zealand just a few days later, I listened to some of Aaron's recordings via his *Subconsciously* app, which helped cement what we'd done in our one-on-one session.

One of my biggest fears is being trapped in a vehicle, so when the producers told us one of the challenges was to be strapped into a helicopter that was lowered to the bottom of a lake and that we couldn't release ourselves until we reached the bottom, I didn't think I'd be able to cope. But I accessed a sense of calm like nothing I've ever experienced before, and I completed the challenge. At the time I thought to myself, I wonder if this is the hypnotherapy…

I honestly don't think I could have gone as far in the show as I did had I not had that hypnosis session beforehand. I was amazed by how quickly and how well the hypnotherapy worked and I'm so excited that Aaron is sharing his knowledge and techniques with more people through this book.

What you'll find in the coming chapters is an introduction to hypnotherapy, and some valuable hypnosis exercises that you can introduce into your own life today. Aaron explained to me that one of the factors that makes hypnotherapy effective is a desire to want to change. You've already shown that desire by picking up this book. Trust me when I say that hypnotherapy can unlock amazing abilities you perhaps didn't even know you had.

So, use the exercises, affirmations and visualisations Aaron shares with you here to start making positive changes in your life. Competing on *Celebrity SAS: Who Dares Wins* has been life-changing for me in many ways, and I know that part of the reason I got so much out of the show is down to the hypnotherapy I received beforehand.

Read this book, use its teachings and start to see your life change for the better.

Cherry Healey
TV Presenter

Prologue

If I had a penny for the amount of times I've been asked how I got into hypnotherapy I would be, well not quite a millionaire, but you get the idea. The truth is I don't really know how I chose to become a hypnotherapist.

One thing I do know is that I'm not a "hypnotist". While this is a similar term to hypnotherapist, it conjures up inaccurate and far-fetched impressions of stage hypnotists and magicians. It also leaves out the all-important word "therapist". For this is what I am – one who provides a specialist form of therapy that relies on communication, interaction and a deep understanding of the human mind.

Throughout my 20+ year career, my intention has been to dispel the myth of hypnosis being "fake" or linked to ticking hand clocks, and to promote its incredible values to mental health, wellbeing and living as full, happy and healthy a life as possible.

For many struggling with mental health challenges, cognitive behavioural therapy (CBT) is the go-to option. This works well for many, but also has its limitations which means there are many more people whom it doesn't serve so well.

The reason CBT doesn't work for everyone is that it requires you to think consciously about the problem, which can exacerbate the issue rather than help solve it. CBT also often requires you to carry out homework and exercises outside of your sessions, which can be tricky to fit into the fast-paced, busy lives many of us have. So, where can these people turn? What alternatives to CBT are available?

The answer is hypnotherapy. Unlike CBT, this creates a mindset transformation subconsciously and automatically. You don't need to consciously think about the problem, triggers or solution. Instead, they evolve naturally.

In the years I've had my practice, I've found that hypnotherapy helps people not to think about the issue that is troubling them or in many instances ruining their lives. Instead, it allows the subconscious mind to be effectively reprogrammed and rewired to think differently. In other words, it shifts a person's mindset and it does so in such a way that often their mindset makes a dramatic U-turn to their benefit.

This shift happens quickly, proactively and in a highly relaxing and uplifting way – through hypnosis sessions. No homework is required, although I recommend my clients listen to my *Subconsciously* app as this helps reinforce the messages I use in our sessions and, therefore, reinforces the change to a positive, confident mindset.

Learning the power of the mind

I had what you could describe as an unusual education, in that my secondary school – James Independent School for Boys – was very

Prologue

unique. It fused a Christian ethos with an ancient Hindu philosophy. I studied there from the age of 12.

Passages of the Bible were emphasised in balance with studying the Gita and the Upanishads from Hinduism. We used to "surrender" knowledge to the one self before and after each lesson by closing our eyes (something that, therefore, became natural to me from an early age) and chanting in Sanskrit (an ancient classical Indian and Hindu language). At the beginning of each lesson, we would chant: "Ommmm Paramart Mona Nama, Utta." We would repeat this chant at the end of each lesson, but replace "utta" with "etti" to surrender the knowledge we had learned to the one self. (Don't ask me what the one self is, I'm still trying to work that one out!).

As well as these regular chants, we would meditate twice daily. Once in the morning for ten minutes and once before school ended. We would chant a mantra (that we weren't allowed to speak about), going from faster to slower and allowing our thoughts to come in and leave without attaching any energy to them. That was the idea anyway. I enjoyed practising it, although occasionally if I was very tired I would use the ten minutes for a nap or perhaps would open my eyes and crack a silently mouthed joke with friends in the class.

But I think these experiences at school were significant and influenced me to go into my vocation as a hypnotherapist. Working on the mind, closing my eyes and looking inside, monitoring the things happening inside the body and inside the mind, had become normal and habitual for me from age 12.

After school, I studied sociology at university and just three to four years after receiving my degree, I set up my practice, originally on Harley Street in London. I had taken an optional extra unit in psychology and health as part of my degree, which had particularly resonated with me, and my desire to help people live happier and more fulfilled lives fitted naturally with the field of hypnotherapy.

Understanding the value of hypnotherapy

Hypnotherapy is still very under researched, but research is increasing, particularly in the US, where it is becoming a more accepted form of therapy. We are lagging far behind in the UK and I think we are missing a trick to harness the potential and great value of hypnotherapy.

This is especially true following the Covid-19 pandemic, which has resulted in the number of people suffering with mental health issues soaring. It seems it is those in the younger generations who are experiencing the greatest mental health fallout from the pandemic.

One thing we do know within the therapeutic community is that disease very often stems, directly or indirectly, from our brain and our mind. Therefore, focusing on providing better and more effective mental health therapies can benefit all of us in a multitude of ways.

To help explain hypnotherapy to those who are unsure, and to help my clients to better understand the neurological processes that occur during hypnosis, I have started using wearable technology in the form of EEG headsets during my sessions. These headsets monitor brainwaves, and it is the beta and theta waves in particular that are important for hypnosis.

However, you do not need to fall into a specific "hypnotised" state to experience these brainwaves. Some of my clients experience vivid visualisations, as well as curious and often wonderful vibrational sensations during hypnotherapy. That said, I have other clients who have found it hard or almost impossible to relax, but who have achieved the same results through their hypnotherapy sessions as my most relaxed patients.

While the EEG headset is a useful tool that I can use to show my clients the varying brainwave patterns that occur during the process of hypnosis, there are other outward signs I look for to indicate that someone is in a hypnotic state. Slower and shallower breathing are good signs that my client has reached a state of heightened awareness where they are more alert than usual, while also being relaxed.

What I have learned over my years as a hypnotherapist is that the depth of the hypnotic state is not the key to a hypnotherapy session's success. It is, in fact, a combination of factors that make hypnotherapy successful: a client's desire to cure the issue they face, the hypnotherapy session itself, the experience of the hypnotherapist and the chemistry between the client and their hypnotherapist.

Does hypnotherapy work?

Ask any of my clients that question and the response will be an unequivocal "yes". What I'm going to share with you in this book are some of the tools that I use with my clients on a daily basis that help them overcome their mental blocks and challenges, and that set them on the path to leading happier, more fulfilled lives.

I want to show you that hypnotherapy isn't an "act", but that it is a very valuable and reliable method for helping you to improve your mental health.

Introduction

What do you think of when you hear the words "hypnosis" or "hypnotherapy"? Are you picturing an unwitting member of an audience brought up on stage and directed to watch a pendulum or watch swinging until they are "hypnotised"? Are you seeing people being directed to do ridiculous things, like pretend to be a chicken? Or maybe you are thinking of people being hypnotised and regressing to past lives.

These are certainly not uncommon associations with the practices of hypnosis and hypnotherapy. However, they are not accurate depictions of the process, nor do they demonstrate the true value of hypnotherapy and the transformative results it can deliver.

Over the years that I've had my practice, I have come across all of the misconceptions and myths you can imagine about hypnotherapy. Part of the challenge is that TV shows from the 1980s involving hypnotists, as well as stage hypnosis shows, mean that many people associate hypnosis with showmanship rather than understanding how it works on a deep psychological level.

The true use of hypnosis in the therapeutic sense couldn't be more different from the image of someone dangling a watch in front of you and lulling you into a hypnotic state. There are many scientific studies that have demonstrated the power of hypnosis, and I believe that as more people in the western world accept practices like meditation, the more people will come to accept hypnotherapy.

Meditation has been shown to relax the brain to the point that we can clear it. Hypnosis takes this a step further by putting an even greater focus on relaxation and in doing so allowing the brain to receive positive hypnotic suggestions which help to literally reprogram your mind to erase bad habits for good, replace negative thoughts with positive ones, and reset your subconscious.

The truth about hypnosis

Neurological research shows that when we undergo hypnotherapy, we are able to access the beta-theta brainwaves that work on a deeper level than the alpha brainwaves we use every day.

When you come for a hypnotherapy session, you aren't sent to sleep – another myth that movies and TV shows have perpetuated. Instead, you enter a state of physical relaxation, but mental alertness. This is a state that you are comfortable in, and it allows me or another hypnotherapist, to use my voice to induce a hypnotic state or implant hypnotic suggestions in your mind.

The key to hypnosis being effective, as you'll see through the examples I share, is that you know you want to change and are open to hypnosis helping you make that change. For hypnotherapy to be effective, I need the consent of my clients and there needs to be chemistry between us. I can't erase anyone's memories or change someone's personality.

Introduction

What I can do, however, is use hypnotherapy as a force for therapeutic good, helping to improve people's mental and physical health one session at a time. Every one of my clients remains in complete control of their minds for the duration of their session. They are welcome to open their eyes during hypnosis and can even move around if they need to.

What the science says…

In case you need hard proof, a study published in the *International Journal of Clinical and Experimental Hypnosis*[1], highlighted that people cannot be made to do things against their will during hypnosis. In fact, clients are usually aware and in control during their sessions. Occasionally they may drift off fully to sleep, but they're able to return to a state of relaxed awareness at any time. They are never out of control.

It is also a myth that only certain people can be hypnotised. My 20+ years of working in this field, as well as other research, indicates that while susceptibility to hypnosis can vary, most people can be hypnotised to some degree. Interestingly, the level of relaxation you reach during hypnosis doesn't seem to affect its results.

Hypnosis results in measurable changes in brain activity. For example, research using neuroimaging that was published in *Psychosomatic Medicine* demonstrated altered brain wave patterns.[2]

---

1   *International Journal of Clinical and Experimental Hypnosis*, Volume 72, (2024), Issue 4

2   *Brain wave patterns accompanying changes in sleep and…* : *Psychosomatic Medicine* (1948). https://journals.lww.com/psychosomaticmedicine/citation/1948/11000/brain_wave_patterns_accompanying_changes_in_sleep.2.aspx.

Another study by Vilfredo De Pascalis found that during hypnosis, the brain is active and engaged rather than in a sleeplike state.[3] You'll notice that many of the studies I cite come from America. This is because much more research has been conducted into hypnotherapy, its benefits and the science behind it, in the USA than in the UK. I believe in the UK we need to spend more time and money on using this incredible tool – hopefully this book will help you better understand hypnotherapy's benefits too.

As a hypnotherapist, I believe it's important to educate people about the reality of hypnotherapy to help dispel any fears or myths that people might have about how hypnosis works and its efficacy as a treatment for everything from overcoming phobias to stopping smoking. The way I see it, hypnotherapy is a collaborative process between the therapist and the client. It is also a process that can dramatically change your life for the better.

Throughout this book, I will share stories from some of my clients to give you real-world examples of how hypnotherapy has helped transform lives. The names and any details that would make any of my clients easily identifiable have been altered to protect their anonymity, but the outcomes they experienced are very real.

I have always prided myself on the privacy, care and service I provide all of my clients, which is why I have taken great care to protect their identities in this book.

---

[3] De Pascalis, V. (2024) 'Brain Functional Correlates of Resting Hypnosis and Hypnotizability: A review,' *Brain Sciences*, 14(2), p. 115. https://doi.org/10.3390/brainsci14020115.

What's holding you back?

But you didn't pick this book up because you wanted to hear about other people's transformations. You're reading this book because you want to undergo a transformation of your own. Really, that's what hypnotherapy is all about – positive transformation.

What I'll share over the coming chapters are some of the most common challenges clients come to me for help with, as well as some tools, like affirmations, meditations and other exercises, that you can use in your daily life to help you create the life you want to live.

Often there is something that holds us back from achieving our full potential, and what I hope to help you do as you read this book is to work out where your mental blocks are and to identify any patterns of behaviour that could be holding you back. Then I'll share some advice about how you can rewire and reprogram your brain to remove negative patterns of behaviour from your life, and replace them with positive alternatives.

So, are you ready to begin your journey towards a happier, more fulfilled and more positive life? Let's get started.

Part One: Building a Foundation for Happiness

There's no escaping the fact that for many of us, what holds us back in life is in our minds. You might have mental blockages you developed in childhood or your teenage years. Perhaps you easily fall into negative thought spirals that derail you and prevent you from seeing the good in life. Do you have imposter syndrome and feel fearful of being "found out"? Or maybe you fixate on the past, raking over experiences and incidents to the point that you forget to live in the present.

That's not to say that having mental blocks or negative thought patterns will make you permanently miserable or depressed. For many of us these are things that crop up from time to time, rather than being the way we think on a daily basis. But just take a moment to think about how often you find your thoughts slipping in a negative direction, and then consider how much better your life could be if you were able to prevent those negative thoughts from taking control.

As a hypnotherapist, I work with people to overcome all of these challenges, and I see my clients becoming happier, more fulfilled and more successful, session by session, as we clear their mental blockages and reprogram negative thought patterns. Being able to recognise when we are mentally "stuck" is important, as it allows us to seek solutions that will set us on a happier path in life.

There is a great deal of research that indicates being positive in life has benefits far beyond improving your mood, as you'll learn throughout the coming chapters. But becoming more positive often requires conscious effort so that we can overcome the mental blocks and negative thought patterns that keep us trapped in a negative state of mind.

In this first part of the book, we'll explore some techniques you can use to help you to overcome mental blockages, reframe negative thoughts, and live more fully in the present moment. This forms the foundation of a happier life for all of us.

Chapter One

Understanding Mental Blockages and Fear of Failure

Mental blockages come in many forms, although often they tie into a fear of failure, which is why we'll address these two topics together in this first chapter. Overcoming mental blockages of any kind is one of the main reasons people seek hypnotherapy, and many of us will have experienced some form of mental blockage in our lives. Perhaps one of the reasons you've picked up this book is because you know you have one or more mental blockages you need to overcome.

It is helpful to understand why we get mental blockages in the first place. After all, when they hold us back from achieving success and realising our potential, it is difficult to understand why our subconscious mind creates them. However, many mental blockages are our mind's way of protecting us from a perceived threat. That perceived threat could be a fear of failing, or a fear of not being good enough.

Common mental blockages include can I succeed? Will I fail often in the workplace? Will I fail in life? Will I be a good parent? Often these tie back to one of the two fears I just identified – fear of failing or not being good enough.

When we are confronted with fear, our rational mind often takes a step back and our subconscious takes over. Without the rational mind to diffuse that fear, we can easily fall into habitual cycles of fear that are driven by our subconscious.

The reason hypnotherapy is so effective for dealing with mental blockages is that it allows you to connect with your subconscious, and uses your own desire to remove those blockages as a tool to dispel the fear that's driving your subconscious response to a given situation.

Hypnotherapists like myself use hypnotic suggestions during sessions as one of the key tools to create change. Hypnotic suggestion is simply the worded suggestions we give a patient when they undergo hypnosis and are in a state of relaxed awareness. Examples of hypnotic suggestions might be, "Your legs are incredibly heavy. They feel as heavy as lead and are too heavy to lift," or "You are starting to feel calmer and much more confident and positive in your everyday life. You are also starting to manage anxiety and stress easily, confidently and effortlessly."

Hypnotic suggestion allows for a healthy, safe, natural and positive reprogramming of the mind. When I talk about reprogramming, I mean programming your mindset via the subconscious with new patterns of behaviour, habits, thoughts and feelings.

The net effect of this reprogramming is a positive change in the neural pathways within our brains. Neural pathways are the networks that send signals throughout our brain and nervous system. Our brains are "neuroplastic", which means they can change.

As a result, our thought patterns, behaviours, habits, and impulses can all be changed via hypnosis and positive hypnotic suggestion via this process of reprogramming. You'll hear much more about all of these topics as you move through this book.

So, through hypnotic suggestion, you rewire and reprogram your subconscious expectation of success, which allows you to live your life without fear of failure and in doing so helps you overcome mental blockages.

Julia's story: held back by the past

Many mental blockages stem from experiences in our childhood or early adulthood. These mental blockages often manifest as self-limiting thoughts and have the power to negatively affect our quality of life and our potential both in the present and the future.

Take my client Julia as an example. She came to see me to help her overcome a crippling fear of public speaking. During our discussion, Julia told me she knew the exact moment that her fear had arisen. She was six years old and was given the task of reciting a poem during an event to mark her and her classmates progressing from nursery into their junior education at school.

Before the event, Julia was excited about the prospect of reciting the poem. But as soon as she stood up in front of the audience of 200 or so people, she froze. She couldn't get a word out and she told me that she felt as though she was having an out of body experience. She felt that everyone's eyes were on her. She left the stage after barely managing to say the last couple of words of the poem, and the trauma has stayed with her ever since.

Julia's fear of public speaking is far from uncommon. I work with many executives, managers and senior leaders who have the same debilitating fear. Some of them find it is a phobia that comes on suddenly. Others, like Julia, can pinpoint a moment in their past that led to their fear.

However, it is not necessary to establish a root cause in order to overcome a mental blockage. In fact, the hypnotic method I've developed – and termed the "Surtees Method" – focuses extensively on positive direct suggestion combined with affirmations and powerful visualisations. You'll notice this in action in the exercises I share throughout this book.

My approach differs from many other hypnotherapists, because they often focus on the past or distant past i.e. childhood and other cognitive areas. I find this can overcomplicate and often waste time in establishing results. Talking about childhood is valuable for many people in therapy, but I recommend psychotherapy for this type of long-term counselling.

The "Surtees Method" focuses on the present and looking forward, rather than looking back. In the 20+ years I've been practising, I've seen clients achieve fast-acting and long-lasting results.

In Julia's case, understanding where her fear of public speaking came from allowed me to provide some additional tailored positive messages for her subconscious mind to adopt to replace the fear. After her hypnotic induction, I told her to press her thumb and middle finger together and to repeat the following: "I am able to easily control anxiety and adrenaline when speaking. I am a confident speaker. I am comfortable with the focus of attention on me."

In all of my work, I focus on the present and moving forward. I believe this is more proactive, productive and effective for my clients. This was what I did with Julia, getting her to focus on how she felt *now*, rather than reliving how she'd felt at age six.

After our sessions, Julia saw a dramatic shift in how she felt about public speaking. She told me she felt at peace with people looking at her and listening to her in meetings, and during major presentations to clients. Through her hypnotherapy, she had learned that the adrenaline she felt was a good thing and could be harnessed positively for public speaking and performance.

Julia also told me she couldn't believe she felt comfortable speaking publicly. In fact, she felt so comfortable she was even ad-libbing and adding extra elements to her presentations and updates. She had effectively made friends with her own mind and her body's adrenaline production. Her previous nervous energy had been translated, through hypnotic suggestion, into a sense of excitement and empowerment. She could be in the moment, with a positive energy and confidence.

Julia's life changed dramatically as a result of her hypnotherapy. She no longer dreaded giving a presentation, delivering an update, or participating in the Monday morning team gathering. She was comfortable leading groups and meetings, and with delivering PowerPoint presentations, where before she was truly terrified.

While the "Surtees Method", which I used with Julia and many of my other clients, works during our sessions, I also recommend my clients reinforce the results by listening to the relevant recordings subconsciously. In my method, I often use headphones that enable brainwave analysis so I can monitor where my clients are in their hypnotic journeys. These headsets are safe, comfortable and becoming more and more accurate, offering incredible insight into the wonder of our brilliant minds.

Understanding and overcoming mental blockages

When self-limiting beliefs and mental blockages keep coming up for us, life feels harder, as though we are trying to wade through thick mud. Mentally we are trapped in a vicious cycle of asking questions of ourselves – "Will I succeed? Will I be a good parent?" – and fearing that the answer to those questions will be "No".

The more we think these thoughts, the more they become habit patterns, building neural connections and pathways in our brains. Humans are creatures of habit in every way, and our minds are no different. The more you think along a certain pathway, the easier it becomes. Often this is purely subconscious.

So, the starting point for overcoming any mental blockage is to question its validity. Notice those thoughts and questions, and stop them in their tracks by asking, "Why do I feel that I can't do this?" or "Why do I feel I am going to fail?" This in itself isn't necessarily enough to overcome the blockage, but it begins the process of thinking differently about your internal monologue.

Once you have identified the blockage, you can seek a solution. The solution I offer my clients – and now you – is hypnosis, as this enables you to reframe and rewire those often untrue thoughts about yourself, your capabilities and your potential. Through this process, I enable my clients to overcome these blockages and succeed in ways they didn't think was possible.

Just as these mental blockages are created by repetitive thoughts, so they are removed by repeated hypnosis, using hypnotic suggestions and messages, as well as affirmations, to help create new neural pathways.

Affirmations are particularly helpful because you can take these outside of the consulting room. They are simple, powerful statements you can tell yourself, such as "I am capable. I will lift this blockage. I will succeed. I will place no more barriers in my own way." By repeating these phrases, you create a new mental pattern that will ultimately help you not only overcome a specific mental blockage, but also to live more of the life you want.

> **Time out: affirmations for overcoming mental blockages**
>
> This is a really simple exercise that you can do right now – and that you can use in your daily life going forward, to help develop new thought patterns.
>
> Take yourself to a quiet, comfortable place where you will not have to concentrate on anything and where you won't be interrupted. Close your eyes and take a nice deep breath. Press your thumb and middle finger together and repeat the following statements to yourself two or three times:
>
> → I no longer allow blockages and barriers to stop me.
> → I believe in myself and I will push on and succeed.
>
> Notice the positive feelings that arise as you say those words. Repeat those affirmations as many times as you feel you need to, then open your eyes and continue reading.

Understanding imposter syndrome

Many people suffer from imposter syndrome, and one of the challenges for those who do is that there is a widely held misconception that there is truth in the idea that they might be an imposter. The subconscious can often overpower the rational mind and create a feeling that you genuinely should not be where you are. However, in my experience, for the vast majority of people, this is false. You should be where you are.

You are not out of your depth. You are capable. But it's not as simple as me (or anyone else) telling you that – which is why hypnotic intervention is so helpful.

The subconscious is such a powerful part of our lives that it can be easy to believe the voice in the back of our mind that's telling us we shouldn't have been promoted, that our boss has made a howling error and that we shouldn't be there. Over time, we begin to believe this voice and it causes imposter syndrome to set in.

I have helped hundreds of people overcome their imposter syndrome, and I can tell you that in all the cases I've dealt with, the belief that they shouldn't be where they are is wholly inaccurate. What we can do, using hypnotherapy, is reset the subconscious so that you become confident in your position and where you are in life, whether personally or in the workplace. Hypnotic intervention and suggestion allows us to reframe your view of reality, to show you that you are there on merit and to allow your confidence in your abilities to shine through. It's no exaggeration to say that challenging imposter syndrome is key to enhancing your life, increasing your enjoyment and quality of life, and improving your mental health.

Like other mental blockages, imposter syndrome stems from a fear of being exposed as not being "fit" for a job, or another role or function you hold in your life. When this persistent fear of being "found out" is present, it often leads to anxiety, low confidence, a low mood and many other issues. Imposter syndrome often prevents people from reaching their full potential because they become scared of progressing in case this puts them in the spotlight.

The term "imposter phenomenon" was originally coined by Clance and Imes in 1978 as part of their seminal study where they interviewed and researched a group of high-achieving women.[4] Despite each woman's clear merits and evidence of their success from a rational perspective, many experienced intense feelings of intellectual fraudulence, and would attribute their achievements to luck or any reason other than their own abilities.

Of course, we know that imposter syndrome is not only experienced by women. There have been numerous other studies into imposter syndrome over the years. Among them was research conducted by Sakulku and Alexander in 2011, which explored perfectionism and imposter syndrome.[5] This research highlighted how perfectionism is often interconnected with imposter syndrome and a fear of failure. In addition, individuals who suffer with imposter syndrome have an inability to recognise success caused and created by themselves.

Common signs that you may be suffering from imposter syndrome are anxiety, depression, a chronic sense of doubt or fear of failure (which can trigger anxiety and depression), low self-confidence and low self-esteem.

If any of this sounds familiar, then I invite you to seek support to overcome these issues. While they may feel insurmountable, I promise you that with the right therapy and therapist, you can change your life for the better, as many of my clients have done.

---

4 Clance, P. R., & Imes, S. A. (1978). The imposter phenomenon in high achieving women: Dynamics and therapeutic intervention. *Psychotherapy: Theory, Research & Practice, 15*(3), 241–247. https://doi.org/10.1037/h0086006

5 Sakulku, J., & Alexander, J. (2011). The Impostor Phenomenon. *International Journal of Behavioral Science, 6*, 73-92.

Natasha's story: overcoming imposter syndrome

Natasha was one such client, whose fear of failure was eating her up inside, almost like a cancer.

She had recently been promoted to a top-level position at the bank she worked at, but a combination of imposter syndrome, a mental blockage and her fear of failure was a toxic cocktail that threatened to engulf her. Her rational mind knew she had the ability to do her new job – she had been promoted on merit and it showed in her past. She was bright, flew through her studies at a prestigious university and she had flown through the ranks at the bank.

But despite all the evidence that she could do this job, and do it well, something from her past was creating a mental blockage. This gave her a crippling fear of failing in the job to which she'd been newly promoted. Adding to the strain she was under, Natasha was going through a messy divorce with an abusive ex-husband, and bringing up two children.

When she first came to see me, she was in a bad way and was ready to leave her job. During our first session, I explained that what she was facing was a common issue that I could help with. I told her that through hypnosis, I would be able to replace her mental block with an expectation of success. Sure enough, over the course of our sessions, that was exactly what happened.

Her subconscious relearned that she is capable, and that she is in her job on merit. It was as though a weight was lifted from her and all of a sudden, instead of being fearful of going to work, she began to enjoy her new role, which resulted in ever greater success. Her new-found sense of self-belief reduced her anxiety. She felt calmer, more empowered and more positive.

Hypnotherapy was a life-changing and life-enhancing experience for her.

The challenge of imposter syndrome

The challenge when you have imposter syndrome is that it is very easy for our subconscious mind to convince us that it is right – that we shouldn't be where we are, or have the levels of success that we do. We begin to believe that inner voice, even when there is substantial evidence to the contrary available to us.

The more we believe that voice, the more imposter syndrome affects our lives. But it's insidious. It isn't always immediately obvious that we have slipped into a constant state of anxiety or fear. We don't always realise how much better our lives could be if we could release those feelings of inadequacy.

Of course, at some point we will notice that we don't feel happy and that we are always worried. This is a clear sign that we need help to challenge imposter syndrome and move beyond it. The good news is that resetting the subconscious can clear these feelings of self-doubt and in doing so allow us to live a more enjoyable, enhanced life with better mental health.

At its core, this hypnotic resetting process is about transforming negative thoughts into positive expectations. I even use positive expectations myself. When I am treating clients, I have the positive expectation that it will be effective, that it will help them and in doing so will reframe and change their lives for the better. Positive expectation can overpower negative thought, and I believe my positive expectation for each of my clients is one of the reasons why I have such a high success rate.

But this process isn't reserved for hypnotherapy sessions. We can all flip negative thoughts into positive expectations at any point during the day.

> **Time out: flipping negative thoughts to positive expectations**
>
> Whenever you notice a negative thought pop into your head, pause and flip the narrative you are telling yourself.
>
> You can use the following statements to help:
>
> → I can do this.
> → I will do this.
> → I can manage anxiety and stress.
> → I expect to feel confident, clear-headed, focused and rebalanced.
>
> When used consistently over time, each of these phrases will help you to rewire, reframe and reset your negative thoughts into positive expectations. The more you do this, the easier it becomes to shift your mind from negative to positive.

This is a technique that I use in my personal life, as well as with my clients. I know, just as you do, that it can be easy to allow negative thought patterns to interfere with my life, but as soon as I recognise those negative thoughts creeping in, I return to my positive affirmations and expectations. This works whether I'm thinking negatively about a personal relationship, my workload, my business, or even my level of focus.

John's story: uniting the subconscious and conscious minds

The reason hypnotherapy is so effective at helping people overcome imposter syndrome is that it unites the subconscious and conscious minds, bridging the gap between the irrational fear that embeds itself in the subconscious and the rational evidence the conscious mind holds to prove that you are, indeed, where you are on merit.

Another of my clients, John, struggled with tremendous feelings of inadequacy and had a classic case of imposter syndrome. He felt he was a fraud, that he would get found out and that there were far more gifted and successful lawyers at the firm for which he worked, despite the fact that he had worked his way up to a very high level.

My first impressions of John were that he was very pleasant, sociable and successful. On talking about how he felt, it was clear that rationally he knew he was bringing in valuable repeat business. Indeed, he was one of the firm's top earners and one of the youngest at his current level. Rationally, he knew there was merit to his success. But his subconscious mind wasn't taking notice of that rational knowledge.

Instead, John's subconscious mind kept telling him that he didn't deserve to be where he was, that it was only a matter of time before someone realised he was a fraud. During our sessions, I used hypnosis to align his rational knowledge of the situation with his subconscious, and reprogram the irrational thoughts that flooded his subconscious.

With each session I saw a physical change in John. His smile returned and, over the weeks, I saw his body language open up. He looked taller, brighter and happier. His eyes regained a spark as he recognised that, on all levels, he was in his position on merit. He also came to realise that not only was he one of the best lawyers in his firm, but he was also one of the best in the city. He gained self-respect through this process and when he left after our final session I saw a lighter, happier, more confident man walk out of the door than the one who had sat before me just weeks earlier.

How to address imposter syndrome

There are many practical ways in which you can address imposter syndrome in your life, like the exercise I shared earlier where you flip negative thoughts to positive ones. However, as with all issues, the first step is acknowledging and understanding the problem. To do so, you have to recognise the symptoms you're experiencing – such as feeling like a fraud, as though you'll be caught out, that others are better than you or that you are in your position due to luck.

Understanding that this is imposter syndrome is an important first step to solving and effectively treating it. Hypnotherapy is particularly effective because it flips the negative into positive; the irrational into rational; the lack of confidence into complete confidence. Recognising that this is a psychological issue that can be fixed is important, because this allows you to open your mind to the possibility that what you believe about yourself isn't true.

Time out: affirmations to tackle imposter syndrome

Take yourself to a quiet, comfortable place where you will not have to concentrate on anything and where you won't be interrupted. Close your eyes and take a nice deep breath. Press your thumb and middle finger together and repeat the following statements to yourself two or three times:

→ I believe in myself.
→ I am confident in my abilities.
→ They know I am here on merit.

Notice the positive feelings that arise as you say those words. Repeat those affirmations as many times as you feel you need to, then open your eyes and continue reading.

Escaping the trap of fear of failure

Fear of failure is perhaps one of the most insidious mental challenges we can face, because it affects our contentment and happiness in life. It is, therefore, important to take steps to overcome your fear of failure as soon as possible. Each day, hour or minute that you fear failure, you are not able to fully enjoy the moments you experience.

Fear of failure often spreads far beyond work. It can set in and impact any area of our lives. A fear of failing as a parent, for example, is very common and one that can mean you don't fully enjoy the time you spend with your family.

Often this fear creeps up on us. It sets in day by day, week by week, month by month. Before you know it, you have wasted potentially years of your life completely needlessly. Fearing failure is a waste of our time and our energy, as well as a blocker to our future happiness and success.

For many of my clients, the fear of failure starts early in their lives, during childhood or their teenage years. Often it has only become worse over time. The first step to addressing it, as with all of these mental blocks and challenges, is acknowledging it. When you recognise that you fear failing, you can stop yourself falling further into the negative downward spiral in which you are in danger of becoming trapped.

If you're reading this and realising that you may be afraid of failing, know that you're not alone. But also know that it is possible to overcome this fear and lean into a life filled with more happiness and success than you currently believe is possible. All I ask is that you're open to trying new things, and that you seek support and a solution without delay.

Be compassionate with yourself. These mental blocks and fears we carry with us through our lives are not anyone's fault, but they are within our power to change. Consider seeking support to overcome your fear of failure as an act of self-care. Go into this process with a willingness to change and have faith that change for the better is indeed possible.

Patrick's story: replacing fear with confidence

When I met Patrick, he was just 25. He had a career at a marketing firm in London, where he had recently started in a new role that was a step up from his previous positions. But Patrick was extremely anxious. He wasn't sleeping, his confidence was through the floor and he was terrified of failing at his new role.

Of course, as with the other stories I've shared in this chapter, there was plenty of evidence to the contrary. Patrick was full of talent. His success was clear through his reviews, the feedback he received from peers and bosses, and his overall performance at work.

However, this was not enough to convince him. His fear of failure combined with imposter syndrome sent him into a negative mental spiral. When he started hypnotherapy with me, I knew we needed to work through the reprogramming and rewiring process to help Patrick embrace all the good in his life and become happier.

As with John, session by session I saw him grow in confidence. Gradually we replaced his negative thoughts with positive expectations. Patrick began to go into situations expecting to succeed, expecting to be in control of his anxiety, and expecting to be confident. His whole focus shifted and this became his new reality. His negative thought pattern that focused on failure became replaced by an expectation of success, which we implanted positively and naturally into his subconscious brain throughout our sessions.

Creating these new habit patterns and new neural connections was possible for Patrick, as it is for all of us, due to the neuroplasticity of our brain. As I touched on earlier, our brains are "neuroplastic", which means they remain able to change and develop new neural network connections throughout our lives. Over the course of several months, Patrick replaced his fear of failure with confidence, self-belief and a positive mindset.

He used many of the tools I'll share throughout this book – visualisation, hypnotic suggestion, anchoring and affirmations. All of this put Patrick on a more positive track in his life and made him happier and more fulfilled.

Simone's story: neuroplasticity in action

I helped Simone when she was 35 years old, but her challenges stemmed from a brain injury she sustained at the age of nine. She was hit by a speeding car, which rendered her unconscious and left her in an induced medical coma for around one month.

Following the accident, Simone turned from a sociable child into an introverted one. She had been the life and soul of the class previously, as well as a very bright child. But when she returned to school she was very withdrawn. In our initial session she told me about the impact her brain injury had had on her memory and balancing emotions. She had withdrawn from society at the age of nine, and that remained the case until she came to see me at 35.

We worked on her desire to re-engage socially with confidence, openness and a greater sense of fearlessness. It was wonderful to see her progress. She messaged me several months after our sessions to highlight the changes she had made in her life and the tremendous progress she had made. She told me she also listened regularly to the recording I made of her final session.

Simone's story highlights the essence of neuroplasticity and shows that our neural network connections can be altered at any point in our lives.

You don't have to accept a fear of failure

Some people may mistakenly believe that it's not possible to overcome a fear of failure. They think this is a natural part of their mindset and, therefore, their life. If you feel like this, then I urge you to reconsider.

I know, based on the many clients I've worked with during my 20+ years as a hypnotherapist, that it is possible to overcome a fear of failure, just as Patrick did. As you've learned, I advocate hypnotherapy and, specifically, my method of hypnotic positive suggestion, to overcome a fear of failure effectively.

All you need is an openness and desire to find a solution to this challenge. Believe me when I say there is no challenge that your brain cannot solve, whether that involves bad habits, negative thought spirals or self-change of any kind.

Chapter Two

Transforming Negative Thoughts into Positive Expectations

In the previous chapter, I talked about how transforming negative thoughts into positive expectations can help you overcome mental blocks, imposter syndrome and a fear of failure. The truth is that this process can benefit all of us. Being able to think more positively and set more positive expectations for ourselves can change our whole way of living on a day-to-day basis.

Hypnotherapy is particularly effective for transforming negative thought loops into positive expectations. In some cases, using tools such as hypnotic suggestion, anchoring and visualisation can flip negative spirals into positive realities and effectively transform someone's life almost overnight.

David's story: developing a new view of the world

One woman came to me to ask if I could help her son, who I'll call David. He had experienced a lot of bullying at school. He was dyspraxic, which made sports challenging for him, and as he was attending an all-boys school. This meant he was singled out and called all kinds of names. Although the school dealt with the bullying, and moved David into a new class, it had a lasting impact and totally destroyed his self-confidence. David was really self-conscious in any group situation, particularly if there were people he didn't know well.

His mother wanted me to have a session with him to help improve his confidence and self-esteem in social environments, before he went on a two-week school trip to Spain. It quickly became apparent that David expected everyone to be horrible to him all the time. Therefore, we worked on transforming that negative thought pattern into a positive expectation that everyone would be kind to him and want to talk to him. This helped him come out of his shell and allowed him to start developing friendships with his new classmates.

My experiences of escaping a negative thought pattern

Some years ago, I was involved in a custody battle to see my youngest son. I faced delay after delay within the court system and could see this was going to stretch on for years. Quite early on in the process I recognised that it was important for me to replace negative thought patterns with positive ones, and to ensure that my focus was not placed on my frustrations, but on what I could control within my life.

I focused on building my hypnotherapy app – *Subconsciously* – and on my passion for promoting and explaining the benefits hypnotherapy offers to the world. I took care of my physical health and even completed a triathlon during the year that the custody hearings were taking place. I also have my own therapists to support my mental health, as well as my app.

Earlier I shared that I was taught to meditate at school. This is a practice I returned to at this time. In doing so, I was able to replace what could have been very destructive, negative thought patterns around the custody battle with a positive focus on growing my business and building my hypnotherapy app, both of which have made me stronger and more successful.

Why are negative thought patterns so insidious?

Imagine a garden where you are trying to grow vegetables or specific flowers. You can't simply plant your vegetables or flowers and leave them to grow, because weeds will also grow in the beds. If you don't regularly remove the weeds, they will end up taking over the space and outcompeting all the flowers or vegetables you've planted.

Negative thoughts do the same to our positive thoughts and expectations. When the odd one springs up, it is easy to ignore. But the more they go unchecked, the more of them there are. One day, you realise they are out of control and are choking the life out of everything positive.

Hypnosis is a great way to help you manage these negative thoughts, keep them under control and eliminate them. Think of rewiring your brain to have a new mindset in a similar way. You're rooting out the weeds in your flower beds and planting new seeds that can grow into nourishing vegetables or beautiful flowers. All you're doing by eliminating negative thought patterns is resetting your inner garden, and unconsciously growing positive thoughts, actions and confident feelings.

Tips for transforming negative thoughts into positive expectations

One way to transform your negative thoughts is to have some reminders that you can replace them with whenever they pop into your head. These can be simple phrases that you can tell yourself, like:

- I can do this.
- I will do this.
- I can manage anxiety and stress.
- I expect to feel confident, clear-headed, focused and rebalanced.

Just repeating those positive expectations can play a major part in transforming a negative thought pattern into a healthier, more positive and more rewarding one. This, in turn, will lead to a more rewarding life.

This is a technique that I regularly use myself, because I know that doing so allows me to rewire, reframe and reset my thought pattern. We will all face periods of challenge in our personal thoughts, whether in relation to managing our workload, a relationship, or in my case creating a training program, building a hypnosis app and even writing this book!

When we hit stumbling blocks in any area of our lives, it can be easy to allow negative thought patterns to interfere. But I have found that reminding myself that what I want to achieve *will happen*, and focusing on positive thoughts really helps me stay in a positive thought pattern.

Always remember that you can change your life. You can change your thought patterns. Bad habits can be replaced with good habits. Change is always possible, any time, any place.

Time out: how to recognise and replace negative thought patterns in your life

Firstly, you have to recognise that your negative thoughts are becoming a habit pattern. When you notice that, you simply need to make time in your day – one minute a day is all it takes – to remind yourself of a positive affirmation.

Take yourself to a quiet, comfortable place. Close your eyes and take a nice deep breath. Press your thumb and middle finger together and repeat the following statements to yourself:

→ I do not need to think negatively. I can flip the negative into a positive.
→ I no longer entertain negative thought patterns. I'm able to replace them with more positive energy thoughts.

It might also help to visualise a balloon, just underneath your belly button. With each inhale, you fill that balloon with particles of positive energy, and with each exhale you deflate the balloon and release tension.

Often the simple act of taking time out of your day to gather your thoughts and recognise that you don't need to stay in that negative spiral is all it takes to bring you back into an entirely different, and much more positive, frame of mind.

How to start noticing your negative thought patterns

There are many common negative thought patterns and we all have the potential to encounter these on a daily basis. I have found that it is useful to make a note of these negative thoughts as they arise. Writing them in a journal is very valuable as it helps the brain to better understand these thoughts and to contextualise them in reality.

As you write down these unhelpful thought patterns, observe them and think about them for what they are. Ask yourself two questions, and write the answers next to the thoughts themselves:

- Are these thoughts useful?
- Are these thoughts true?

More often than not, you'll realise that the negative thoughts you're experiencing aren't true or useful. This is a simple process by which you can hold those thoughts up to the light, analyse them and then recognise them for what they are – false, unhelpful thoughts that are a waste of your time and energy.

Next to each of the negative thoughts you've noted, you can write down responses such as, "Not true", "This is not who I am", "I am not my negative thoughts". Then you can flip those negative thoughts to help you focus on the positives. Even telling yourself, "Today I flip negative for positive, anxious for calm, low confidence for high confidence," can help you begin to reframe your thoughts in a more positive way.

Greg's story: performance anxiety

One client of mine, Greg, had a challenge that is all too common and one that I see regularly in my practice – he could not get the idea that he could not perform sexually out of his mind. He told himself he was a failure to the point that he constantly felt anxious when he was in bed with his partner. This would mean he lost his erection and was unable to perform. It was a classic example of performance anxiety causing erectile dysfunction.

Over the course of several sessions, I used hypnotic suggestions to reprogram Greg's mind to give him positive, confident thoughts. I created positive anticipation and expectation that he could easily gain and maintain an erection, and that he could enjoy being in the moment during sex, anxiety free. After several sessions, he revealed that his erectile dysfunction had gone. It was a massive relief he could enjoy being intimate with his partner again.

The power of positive thinking

Our minds and our bodies are closely linked. Really, they are two sides of the same coin. Positive thinking has been scientifically shown to help with many aspects around quality of life and physical health, as well as mental health.

One study conducted by Lisa R. Yanek, M.P.H, an expert at John Hopkins, found that people with a family history of heart disease who also had a positive outlook on life were one-third less likely to have a cardiovascular event (aka a heart attack) within five to 25 years, compared to those with a negative outlook.[6]

The researchers also revealed that in the general population, those with a positive outlook were 13 per cent less likely to have a heart attack, or other coronary event, than those with a negative outlook. To determine whether someone had a positive or negative outlook, the researchers looked at each person's cheerfulness,

---

6   *The power of positive thinking* (2024). https://www.hopkinsmedicine.org/health/wellness-and-prevention/the-power-of-positive-thinking.

energy levels, anxiety levels and satisfaction with their health and overall life.

Although they didn't find conclusive proof in this study, the researchers also noted that they suspect a positive outlook can mean you're better protected against the inflammatory damage of stress.

Another study from the Harvard T.H. Chan School of Public Health found that optimistic women had a significantly reduced risk of dying from major causes of death – including cancer, heart disease, stroke, respiratory disease and infection – over an eight-year period.[7]

The data for this research came from 70,000 women. Researchers found that the most positive thinking individuals had a 16 per cent lower risk of dying from cancer, a 38 per cent lower risk of dying from heart disease or respiratory disease, a 39 per cent lower risk of dying from stroke, and a 52 per cent lower risk of dying from infection.

Of course, positive thinking isn't a complete panacea, and thinking positively alone can't solve all of our problems or guarantee health or success in life. However these studies, and many more like them, show that there is a strong correlation between positive thinking and improved physical health.

What we need to recognise is that, while positive thinking isn't a magic solution for all situations, it does have its benefits. When we can balance positive thinking with realistic expectations, we improve our chances of succeeding. When we combine positive thinking with practical efforts, planning, perseverance and

---

[7] *Optimism may reduce risk of dying prematurely among women* (2020). https://www.hsph.harvard.edu/news/press-releases/optimism-premature-death-women/.

resilience, we are even more likely to succeed in whatever we focus on in life.

Belinda's story: lifting the weight of anxiety

I will never forget Belinda, who came to see me with a serious case of health anxiety, as well as a severe fear of flying. While these two challenges were interrelated in some ways, they also manifested separately. Therefore, we treated each individually over the course of four sessions.

What is interesting about Belinda, and what is true for many of my clients, is that she is highly rational, very confident and incredibly successful as a businesswoman. But when it came to the health of her son, she was enveloped in a constant fear. Every cough, sneeze or sniffle would send waves of adrenaline through her body.

If she ever received a call from his school, it would be catastrophised. She was always expecting tragic news. Belinda recognised that this wasn't healthy for her or her son.

Session by session, we worked on uniting Belinda's rational and irrational minds so that when the school called or her son coughed, she didn't feel instant panic or a flood of adrenaline. Instead, she could respond in a level-headed, rational way, as she did in every other area of her life. The change was dramatic. Removing these negative thought patterns around her son's health lifted a gigantic weight of dread from her shoulders that she had been carrying with her on a near-daily basis.

We worked through the same process to tackle her fear of flying so that she was no longer filled with a sense of dread at being stuck inside a plane for any number of hours. Belinda faced flights with a calmness and confidence she had lacked before. She knew there was nothing to fear, and her mind now accepted that to be true, allowing her to control her physical response to being in that situation.

Time out: positive affirmations for positive thoughts

Starting your day with positive affirmations is a great way to begin to reprogram your brain to focus more on the positive aspects of life and to dwell less on the negative. Come up with a few statements about yourself that set a positive tone for your day. Here are some suggestions to help you get started:

→ I am strong, positive and capable.
→ I believe in myself.
→ I am confident in myself.

Take some time each morning to repeat each of those affirmations two to three times. Practise with me now. Press together your thumb and middle finger on each hand, close your eyes and take a couple of deep breaths.

Repeat each of those affirmations twice. Take a couple more deep breaths, open your eyes and continue reading.

If you can incorporate that practice into your morning, you'll start to notice subtle, but positive, changes in your days. If you have a habit of scrolling through the news in the morning, how about replacing that time with the affirmations practise I just shared? Do it for a week and see how you feel.

Other strategies for positive thinking

Another strategy that is highly effective at making you think more positively is adopting a daily gratitude practice. Take a few minutes each morning or evening to write down three things you are grateful for, allowing yourself to focus on what's good and abundant in your life.

Meditation is also an important part of being mindful, so look at where you can incorporate short meditation exercises throughout your day. Taking a few deep breaths, meditating for a few minutes, sitting upright somewhere you are not going to be distracted for that short time, and pausing to fully engage with the present moment is a great way to help you be more positive.

Positive visualisation is another key strategy, and this is integral to all of the work I do. I recommend that you spend a few minutes a day visualising positive outcomes for your goals and challenges. Imagine yourself succeeding. Experience the positive emotions associated with those successes. Also use this as an opportunity to engage in positive self-talk. Monitor your own internal dialogue, and challenge negative thoughts immediately. Replace them with positive ones, like those I've already shared in this book. Think of empowering statements similar to affirmations. So, instead of, "I can't do this" or "I will fail", say, "I believe in myself", "I can do this", and "I will succeed".

Another strategy that is easily overlooked in our busy days is performing small daily acts of kindness. Make this a habit and consciously perform small acts of kindness each day. This can generate a dopamine boost which will really help your mood and reinforce a more positive outlook on life. It's also a great way to appreciate being in the moment.

Physical activity and exercise is another natural mood booster that you can tap into. Find a way to incorporate exercise into your daily routine. This could be a morning jog, yoga, pilates, hitting the gym, or an evening walk.

At the end of each day, take a few moments to reflect on your positive experiences or accomplishments. This can help reinforce positive memories and end your day on a positive note. It's also great to create a positive environment and surround yourself with things that inspire and uplift you. That might mean some strategically positioned motivational quotes, playing cheerful music, having an organised space, or displaying pictures of people, places or things that you love.

Ultimately, being in a positive environment makes it much easier to embrace the positives in your life.

Sustaining a positive mindset

All the strategies I've just shared will be most effective when done consistently, and this is the key to sustaining a positive mindset. However, we all have periods when life is stressful or challenging, which can make it more difficult to remain upbeat and optimistic.

In addition to the strategies I've just shared, there are some other practical steps you can take when you're facing a particularly challenging or difficult time.

- **Set realistic goals:** Break any larger challenges into smaller, more manageable ones. This is really important for you to feel as though you are continuing to move forward. Celebrate small accomplishments along the way to build momentum.
- **Keep a gratitude journal:** Writing down a few things you're grateful for each day can help shift your focus from the challenges you face and anything you perceive as going wrong to the positive aspects of your life and what's going right.

- **Maintain your relationships:** A social support network is crucial during challenging times. Don't shut out your friends, family or partner. Open up and share your feelings, thoughts and experiences with those you trust. This is just as important as being willing to listen to and support them in return.
- **Make time for physical activity and regular exercise:** This can boost your mood and energy levels. Walking, running, yoga, pilates, going to the gym or doing any form of exercise you enjoy can help reduce stress and improve your overall wellbeing. It also improves your ability to be resilient in the face of challenges and tough times.
- **Have a daily routine:** This can provide a sense of stability. Stability helps to structure your day and keep you focused and productive.
- **Limit doom scrolling:** Cut back on (or eliminate) any time spent checking negative news. Constant exposure to negative news can heighten anxiety, low mood, stress and insecurity. Consider limiting your news intake to specific times of the day for a specific amount of time.
- **Engage in hobbies and activities that bring relaxation and joy:** These could be reading, dancing, cooking, listening to music or any other interest. Any activity you enjoy is a great mood booster and a good way to increase your dopamine, giving you the feel-good factor.
- **Seek therapy and talk to trained counsellors:** This is an effective solution for many, as is focusing on what you can control. Concentrate on actions and decisions within your control, because worrying about things you can't change is a waste of energy and a time drain. Channel your energy into areas where you can make a difference.
- **Be kind to yourself:** Demonstrate self-compassion during difficult times. Acknowledge your feelings without judgement. Give yourself permission to take breaks and care for your mental and physical health.

- **Use hypnosis on a regular basis:** I tell my clients to listen to the relevant hypnosis recordings on my *Subconsciously* hypnosis app. Try to make it a consistent habit to listen, as this will help with the reprogramming and rewiring of your mindset. Using hypnotic suggestion to make new neural connections promotes greater resilience and positivity during difficult times in life.

Why is sustaining positivity so important?

How positive we feel about our lives is a kind of litmus test for the quality of our lives, the enjoyment we get from our lives and how able we are to live in the moment. As we've seen, positivity is extremely important for both our mental and physical health.

We know positive thinkers experience lower levels of depression and anxiety than those with a more negative outlook, that they cope much better with stress, and have much greater resilience when faced with challenges and adversity. Positive thinkers also have a more dynamic and proactive approach to challenges and problem-solving. This further negates and neutralises the impact of stress and negative emotions.

In addition, more optimistic people have stronger immune systems, helping them to fight off diseases much more efficiently and quickly. As I mentioned earlier, being optimistic is also associated with a lower risk of death from cancer, heart disease, respiratory illness and other conditions.

Without positive thinking it's much easier to fall into spirals of apathy or develop a low mood, negative thinking, and even become depressed or have suicidal thoughts. Negative emotions are often associated with chronic stress, which can create additional anxiety, lower your mood, and weaken the immune system. Negative thinking and more pessimistic thinking also relates to a higher risk of premature death from various diseases. Additionally, negative thinking can shorten life expectancy by promoting unhealthy behaviours as well as aggravating health issues.

Promoting positive thinking is what I do in every session I have with my clients. In fact, I incorporate affirmations around positive focus and feeling greater positive energy in life with every client I see because no matter who I'm treating, or what issue they face, finding more positivity will always be beneficial.

It's very clear to me from my experience over 20 years as a hypnotherapist, as well as from numerous scientific and psychological studies, that sustaining and promoting positivity is crucial for having a good quality of life. Being positive allows us to live a healthier and happier life, enhances mental resilience, makes tackling problems and challenges in life easier, improves physical health and increases our lifespans.

Changing a negative for a positive is essentially the bread and butter in my hypnosis practice. One of the most wonderful parts of my job is seeing people go from thinking very pessimistically and experiencing severe anxiety, to thinking more positively and transforming their lives as a result. They sleep better. They have better relationships with those around them. They are happier in themselves. This is the power of positive thinking, and illustrates why we should all do what we can to bring more positivity into our lives.

Chapter Three

Letting Go of the Past and Being Present

When we live in the past, it can create obstacles to leading a fulfilled life and realising our full potential. Letting go of the past is crucial for living a happier life, because we need to be in the present. This is where we *actually* live life. Similarly, living in the future isn't fully living either, as by doing so you're not fully engaging with real life in the here and now.

We need to learn to appreciate the beauty of the moment, the breath, the heart beating, being alive, feeling the sun on our skin and the breeze on our face, smelling flowers like roses and daffodils. When we can appreciate these small things, we are fully living in each moment of our lives.

The problem with living in the past, in particular, is that it saps our energy, vitality, happiness and contentment. It impacts life in every way and stops us from living more full, healthier and happier lives. The reason being that if we are living in the past, we're not actually living – instead we're focusing on another life, one that we don't have control over.

I know the dangers of living in the past all too well, having experienced this myself. I felt retrospective jealousy with my partner when we discussed previous sexual partners and relationships. I found myself in a negative thought loop, wanting to know every detail even though rationally I knew I didn't want to know every detail.

I realised that if I wanted to have a happier and healthier relationship – as well as a happier and healthier life – I had to not only feel good about putting her past where it belonged, in the past, but I also had to learn to live in the present and enjoy it for all that it was. Doing so, by using many of the techniques I'm sharing with you throughout this book, helped me not only become happier in myself, but also strengthened our relationship.

Christine's story: the impact of past trauma

When Christine came to see me, she hadn't driven a car for 35 years. She explained that she couldn't get behind the wheel after experiencing the trauma of almost dying in a car accident. She was in her early 20s at the time, travelling from London to Manchester. During the journey, she fell asleep at the wheel and awoke as she was hurtling towards the back end of a large HGV. She swerved into the next lane, narrowly avoiding colliding with other vehicles. She was lucky that it was early in the morning, when there were fewer cars on the road.

She didn't initially experience a great deal of trauma and continued driving for a few months, but then the post-traumatic stress of the incident hit her. For 35 years she hadn't driven, and she struggled to relax as a passenger.

This was why she came to see me. Her husband was frustrated that whenever they needed to drive to other parts of the country, which they did often, she would flinch and jump whilst on the motorway for no reason, where no danger existed. Her past trauma was, therefore, creating great tension in her relationship with her husband.

She even told me that she would often fly from London to Manchester, to avoid the drive. 35 years on, she wanted to deal with that trauma. Over the course of our sessions we lifted her trauma using a combination of hypnotic suggestion, affirmation and visualisation to help Christine become a calm passenger, who could travel with any driver, on any motorway, under any conditions, without flinching.

This process enabled her rational mind to be heard. It gave her the confidence that she was safe, and that she could trust the driver of the car. After our sessions, she has not only been able to stop spending a fortune on flights, but can also enjoy the convenience of jumping in the car for a journey.

Other ways to release past trauma

Alongside hypnosis, there are many other therapies that can help you deal with trauma. These include psychotherapy, eye movement, desensitisation and reprocessing. Meditation is always helpful, and I'll talk more about meditation and how to develop a meditation practice shortly. The reason it's beneficial is that it makes you focus on being present in the moment, which reduces anxiety and promotes emotional regulation.

Here are some specific ways to help you deal with past trauma:

- **Body scan meditation:** This helps you become more aware of physical sensations. It can also uncover areas where trauma is actually stored in the body.

- **Writing your experiences and feelings down:** This is a very important part of dealing with trauma from a practical point of view and can help you to start releasing the trauma.
- **Art therapy:** This is helpful for many people. It involves using drawings, paintings and other forms of creative expression to release emotions.
- **Regular physical activity and exercise:** This is always great for improving your mood, and releasing physical tension.
- **Breath work:** This is a practical way in which you can regulate your nervous system and facilitate trauma release. John Hopkins University is conducting a pioneering study as I write this about the effects of holotropic breathwork on veterans with PTSD.[8] Holotropic breathwork helps individuals access deep emotional states. It is believed it can facilitate significant trauma release without the need to actually relive traumatic events explicitly.

Mindfulness for our emotional and mental health

Mindfulness is the practice of being fully present and engaged in the current moment. This means being aware of your thoughts, feelings and sensations without judgement, and focusing on the present rather than dwelling on the past or anticipating the future. Focusing on the here and now is very beneficial for our mental and emotional health.

Mindfulness has also been found to reduce stress by helping people to manage unwanted stresses and promoting relaxation. By focusing on the present moment, mindfulness can interrupt the cycle of stress, anxiety, repetitive thoughts and, indeed, intrusive

---

8 *Breathwork study on PTSD* (no date). https://www.recapturetherapture.com/ptsd.

thoughts. In doing so it can reduce the physiological effects of stress on the body.

It also helps to improve emotional regulation. Mindfulness increases our awareness of our emotions, allowing us to recognise and respond to feelings in a more balanced way. Hypnotherapy and hypnosis also allows a greater ability to control the mind and feel more relaxed, calm, confident and in control. Unlike mindfulness that you practise yourself, hypnosis and hypnotherapy occurs without you actually having to think about your emotions or thoughts because the reprogramming and resetting is automatically happening through your therapist's words.

One notable study on the importance of mindfulness for our mental and emotional health came from Khoury et al. (2015), where they found mindfulness-based techniques were moderately effective in reducing stress, depression, anxiety and distress.[9]

A further randomised and controlled trial by Teasdale et al. used a mindfulness-based cognitive therapy (MBCT) to reduce relapse rates among recurrently depressed patients. The MBCT helped them recognise and disengage from negative thought patterns. In 55 of the patients who had experienced three or more previous depressive episodes, relapse rates fell from 78 per cent to 36 per cent with the use of MBCT.[10]

---

[9] Khoury B, Sharma M, Rush SE, Fournier C. Mindfulness-based stress reduction for healthy individuals: A meta-analysis. J Psychosom Res. 2015 Jun;78(6):519-28. doi: 10.1016/j.jpsychores.2015.03.009. Epub 2015 Mar 20. PMID: 25818837.

[10] Ma SH, Teasdale JD. Mindfulness-based cognitive therapy for depression: replication and exploration of differential relapse prevention effects. J Consult Clin Psychol. 2004 Feb;72(1):31-40. doi: 10.1037/0022-006X.72.1.31. PMID: 14756612.

However, hypnosis and hypnotherapy allows this to occur on a greater level through inducing a trance, and facilitating the rewiring process in a concentrated and deliberate way. While meditation is beneficial, it does not support rewiring in such a direct way.

Tom's story: turning the narrative around

When Tom came to me he had a high degree of health anxiety. In his case, he had reason to be anxious because his heart was not in good shape. He had around a four-inch section of calcium in one of the main arteries in his heart. The prognosis did not look particularly promising.

His doctors had told him that in his current state, he had a 50 per cent chance of suffering a heart attack within the next ten years, and a less than ten per cent chance of surviving it if he did. However, his heart surgeon also told him that if he stuck to a plant-based diet, regularly exercised, walked daily, and reduced his levels of stress and anxiety that he could live quite happily for another 10 to 20 years without any issues.

The problem was that Tom had disappeared down a Google hole. He had spent too long doom scrolling, focusing on the negatives of his situation and reading up on all the stats that involved death. Of course, this did nothing to alleviate his stress or anxiety. His behaviour was pushing him ever closer to the heart attack that was causing him such anxiety.

When we started our sessions, we focused on the positives, based on what his heart surgeon had told him. Through our sessions, we changed his outlook to be dramatically positive. Tom felt calmer and his hope was restored. He started to live again, instead of resigning himself to a heart attack and an early death. He developed positive habits – eating and enjoying a plant-based diet, enjoying walking ten miles a day, and enjoying returning to positivity. Tom was able to live in the moment, enjoy life, and be calmer and more optimistic as a result.

Embracing meditation to improve mindfulness

There are many practices that can help your mind stay in the moment, but one that helps many people is meditation. That said, I know that a lot of people find meditating hard because their mind drifts and rarely feels "clear". This leads to frustration and can make you believe that you "can't" meditate. But nothing could be further from the truth.

I often tell my clients that it doesn't matter if their mind is drifting and wandering during our sessions or when they are meditating at home. The key to getting the benefit from meditation is to be able to take in positive messages, even if your mind is daydreaming or entering random thought loops.

When you make time to meditate, do so with the intention of having a desire for a change, to destress or whatever reason you have for meditating at this moment. Even if your conscious mind is wandering, your subconscious mind will be listening and taking those messages of intention on board.

This is why listening to hypnotherapy recordings, like the ones you'll find in my app *Subconsciously*, is beneficial, because those messages will penetrate through to your subconscious even if you're thinking about other things while listening to them.

Again, this doesn't have to be a long process. Even if you only take two to three minutes each day to listen to some positive affirmations, it can help reset your brain and create new neural pathways.

What does hypnosis do to the brain?

Studies into the neuroplasticity of the brain show how these neural connections can be reset through hypnotherapy, staying present and changing bad habits for good ones. World authority on neuroscience and the brain David Spiegel has spent decades using brain scanning equipment on people receiving hypnotherapy, and such studies have revealed the changes that occur in brainwaves under hypnosis.[11]

The prefrontal cortex, which is the part of the brain towards the front known as the "personality centre" where we process moment-to-moment thoughts/feelings from our surroundings, and the insula, which is the small part of the brain situated centrally and buried deep, play an important role in emotional processing, sensory processing, decision making and empathy. During hypnosis, the connections between these important parts of the brain increase. This is significant, because the prefrontal cortex and insula are responsible for our brain-body connection, which helps the brain process and control what's going on in the body.

This study also found hypnosis reduced connections between the prefrontal cortex and the default mode network, which is the network of brain regions that are active when the brain is resting or not engaging in a task or job of some kind. During hypnosis daydreaming and random wandering thoughts are common, as is having barely no thoughts at all. This type of dissociation between action and reflection is typical of patients undergoing hypnotherapy. It allows for a greater automatic effortless focus

---

11   Williams S.C.P. (July 2016), *Study identifies brain areas altered during hypnotic trances*, Stanford Medicine, https://med.stanford.edu/news/all-news/2016/07/study-identifies-brain-areas-altered-during-hypnotic-trances.html

on the hypnotic suggestions and whatever the hypnotherapist needs to communicate.

It's important to remember that whilst words like disassociation and even prefrontal cortex sound a little scary, hypnosis is far from scary. In fact, it's often very pleasurable, highly relaxing and you remain awake and in control throughout. Unlike meditation, there is no need to try to clear your mind or to worry about the thoughts you may or may not have when you undergo hypnosis. In fact, random thoughts, images and feelings are not only fine and normal, but can even help deepen the pleasant state of hypnosis.

In addition, the researchers observed a decrease in activity around the dorsal anterior cingulate – a smallish curved area just behind the prefrontal cortex. This area deals with many important functions in humans, and is referred to as the salience network. It deals with a multitude of sensory information about ourselves, the world and people around us. During hypnosis the activity here is reduced to allow for physical relaxation and focused awareness. In other words, you become more absorbed in the experience itself and, therefore, outside stimuli become less and less noticeable or significant during this time.

Time out: staying in the moment

I'd love you to put the book down and do a short exercise. Go somewhere comfortable – perhaps lie down on a bed or a sofa, or sit back in a comfortable chair. Close your eyes and focus on what you can feel. Notice the weight of your body as you take a nice deep breath. Press your thumb and middle finger together and repeat the following affirmations:

→ I am able to stay present and enjoy being in the moment.
→ I am able to enjoy being in the moment.
→ I am able to enjoy being in the present.

Now imagine yourself in a beautiful space in nature. There's blue sky above you and you have a beautiful scene in front of you. The climate is just right for you. You feel comfortable. Now repeat the following:

→ I am present here, in the now.

As you say those words one, two, three times, imagine you have a smile on your face – this is a smile of positive presence. It's what you get when you are truly present, truly here and living in the moment. When you feel ready, open your eyes gently, take a deep breath and continue reading.

How can mindfulness help if you're struggling with anxiety or stress?

Both hypnotherapy and mindfulness can be very effective for people struggling with anxiety or stress. Practising mindfulness helps you to become much more aware of your thought patterns, allows you to disengage from repetitive negative thinking, and teaches you how to replace it with more positive, useful, beneficial thinking.

By focusing on the present moment, you reduce your tendency to dwell on the past or worry about the future. This is key for building resilience, which you develop by cultivating an accepting attitude towards life's challenges. Improved resilience helps you to cope better with stress, reducing the overall impact of anxiety and stress in your life.

Mindfulness, along with hypnotherapy, also improves your sleep quality by reducing the mental and physical tension that often accompanies stress and anxiety. We all know that sleep enhances our overall wellbeing and reduces the symptoms of anxiety and stress, so finding techniques that help us sleep better has many positive knock-on effects.

What it means to live in the moment

To truly live in the moment means fully engaging with the present experience and letting go of any kind of preoccupation with the past, regrets, or future stresses and worries. It involves paying close attention to what is happening right now – your thoughts, feelings, sensations, surroundings – without judgement or distraction. As Eckhart Tolle wrote in his classic, *The Power of Now*, "Time isn't precious at all, because it is an illusion. What you perceive as precious is not time, but the one point that is out of time: the Now. That is precious indeed. The more you are focused on time — past and future — the more you miss the Now, the most precious thing there is."[12]

Eckhart Tolle also talked about an intense period of anxiety and suffering that he experienced around the age of 29 when he thought, "I cannot live with myself any longer." That thought kept repeating itself until he became aware of what a peculiar thought it was. "If I cannot live with myself there must be two of me, the I and the self that I cannot live with, maybe I thought only one of them is real."

This inspired a period of investigation, during which he was able to see that the mind was creating the suffering, while the I who was observing it, was the "I am". In recognising this, he recentred and refocused on the mind, being fully in the here and the now.

---

12   Tolle, E. (1999) *The power of now: A Guide to Spiritual Enlightenment.* New World Library.

The point to take away from Tolle's writing is that because you are not your mind alone, you can refocus the mind. You can disidentify from the mind, and you can channel and focus your mind. Every time you do that, the power of consciousness grows stronger, and the quality of your life is enhanced.

Being in the now is incredibly beneficial. It does so many things, from improving emotional regulation and enhancing your ability to manage emotions effectively, to improving your attention, and retraining the brain – the mind's focus – one thing at a time.

When you can improve your focus, you also improve your productivity, quality of work, efficiency, concentration and attention. But perhaps the greatest benefit of focusing on the now, the most precious thing we have, is that by experiencing the present moment fully, you can find joy and satisfaction even in simple everyday activities. Being fully present in the now also strengthens your relationships – personal and professional – by enabling you to develop far more meaningful connections, have deeper communication and have more enjoyable interactions with others.

Luke's story: relationship rumination

I'll never forget Luke, who for eight years had been struggling to get over his ex-partner. They had broken up, got back together, and eventually broken up again. Their final breakup had been her decision, not his. Luke couldn't stop himself ruminating on what had gone wrong.

He was ruminating over hundreds of potential outcomes, getting fixated on variables, regrets, what-ifs, maybes, should haves, could haves and would haves. All of this questioning was driving him to wonder what the point in life was.

When he came to me, he was caught up in the worst types of human emotion – stress, anxiety, regret, sadness, depression. He had a nasty level of jealousy over her new boyfriend. He even felt unable to return to his hometown to visit his parents because of all the triggering memories this led to of his time with his former partner.

Over the course of our ten sessions together, I saw the hypnosis was helping him, but only to a limited degree. Luke couldn't let go and fully forget his ex, and there was a reluctance to try to meet a new partner himself. He was still hung up on regrets and although our time together certainly helped and gave him new coping mechanisms, they weren't as effective as they could have been if Luke had truly and completely desired to improve his life.

Hypnosis doesn't work for everyone, and in Luke's case while it was helpful it wasn't as effective as it has been for many of my other clients. This is largely because of the mental barriers Luke put up to the process being effective.

Live for the moment, not in the past

Luke is a good example of someone who is living well and truly in the past, and whose life has suffered for it in the present. He couldn't move on from the heartbreak of his relationship ending, and as a result he lived a sad and regretful life, wasting his valuable time on this Earth.

People who neglect to live in the moment suffer from increased anxiety and stress. They tend to waste their energy ruminating on the past or situations they have no control over, which can lead to burnout, low moods, depression and worse.

Failing to live in the moment – and failing to realise that you're not living in the moment – can create a cycle of negative thinking that reduces your ability to regulate your emotions and decreases the satisfaction you have with your life. You may feel as though life is passing you by.

As I've already said, our mental and physical health is inextricably linked. Spending your time focusing on the past in such a negative way can also result in physical health issues ranging from a weakened immune system or frequent illness, to digestive issues or even chronic health conditions.

Not being present during interactions with others can put a huge strain on our relationships too, leading to misunderstandings, poor communication and a lack of emotional connection with others.

In the simplest terms, when we don't live in the moment we miss out on the simple pleasures and joys in life. Experiencing the here and now in all its deep, rich, powerful wonder is one of the most precious gifts – if not the most precious gifts – we as humans can give ourselves on this planet.

Time out: focusing on the present

This technique can help you to focus on the present. It is a hypnotic technique that incorporates a breathing exercise.

Before you begin, make sure you're in a fairly comfortable place, preferably sitting or lying down. Your back should be quite straight, but not rigid. Sink into your position. Let your eyes close and take a nice deep breath.

Imagine a balloon just underneath your belly button. As you inhale, imagine white particles of relaxing energy filling up the balloon. You're inhaling relaxation as the balloon inflates, exhaling tension as the balloon deflates. Anchor this comfortable feeling now by pressing together your thumb and middle finger.

Observe the breath, without trying to change it, and without any judgement.

Notice your breathing's natural rhythm. Notice any sounds around you, whatever sounds they may be. Notice the smells. Focus on the here and now. Remember right now there is only here, now, at this moment. Even with your eyes closed you can notice perhaps some colours, shades, tones, textures. Perhaps some of the light around you is still just about seeping into the very edges of your eyes.

Notice how your body feels. Let go of any tension, head to toe. Notice the weight of your body, whether you're sitting or lying. Notice the air brushing against your skin, as well as the tiniest of movements, sensations and feelings.

In your mind, repeat to yourself: "I am here, in the now, present, living now, in the moment. I learn to live more and more in the now. I am in the now, here and now, living, breathing, experiencing. I give great respect to now. I acknowledge and give great respect to the here and now."

Repeat those words to yourself once or twice. Then let your eyes open and take a nice deep breath, while keeping your focus on the present.

Part Two: Regaining Control and Breaking Bad Cycles

Now that you've started the process of building foundations for a happier and more positive life, you can begin to look at what patterns of behaviour need to change in order to allow you to achieve your full potential and live the life of your dreams.

Regaining control of your life starts by identifying your negative habit patterns and doing the work necessary to break bad cycles of behaviour. Many of us will face self-confidence issues at some stage in our lives, and a lack of self-confidence in our abilities can hold us back from achieving our potential. So, we'll begin this part of the book by exploring where these confidence issues arise from and how we can overcome them.

Addictions are particularly challenging negative patterns of behaviour to break, but as you'll see in Chapter 5, not only is it possible to break an addiction, but it's also possible to replace that addiction with a much more positive set of behaviours.

Subconsciously

Finally in this part of the book we will look at one of the main challenges we all face when attempting to achieve our goals – procrastination. There are many practical ways in which we can set ourselves up for success and overcome procrastination, which I'll share with you in Chapter 6.

Chapter Four

Overcoming Self-Confidence Issues

A lack of self-confidence can have a negative impact on both our careers and personal lives. Often when we suffer with confidence issues it impacts our self-worth, how we value ourselves and how we assess our abilities. When we have low self-confidence in ourselves, it can stop us progressing, whether that means holding us back from advancing in our careers or preventing us from moving on with our lives in some other way.

In our personal lives, a lack of self-confidence often has a dramatic impact on our relationships and prevents us from establishing friendships or making connections with romantic partners. It can mean we procrastinate in many aspects of our lives, and as a result that we end up only living half the life that we could.

Sometimes, having self-confidence is spoken about in negative terms. One of the most common misconceptions I encounter about building self-confidence and self-esteem is that it involves you becoming an arrogant person. Self-esteem does not and should not involve arrogance. It stems from how you view yourself and your world.

For too many of us, our self-esteem and sense of self-worth is damaged early in life through childhood traumas, being ridiculed or bullied, or even from negative comments made by our parents. In some cases, abuse – physical, emotional or sexual – can be behind low self-esteem.

Whatever has triggered your self-confidence and self-esteem to drop, know that you can build it back up by reprogramming, rewiring and reframing the thoughts in your mind that contribute to your self-esteem, no matter what has happened in the past. Hypnotherapy is especially good at helping people to develop their self-esteem in a fast, proactive, positive and painless way.

Danielle's story: stepping into the spotlight

Danielle came to see me when she was on the verge of giving up on her vocation and passion of being a soloist ballerina. She was in her early 20s and had great potential, but many around her had sown doubt in her mind for years. At school, she was subjected to ultra-strict, judgemental teaching methods and was regularly told that she was "too big" to be a ballerina. All of this demolished her confidence and created lingering worries about her abilities and even her physical shape.

During our first session, I could see she was riddled with self-doubt. But we set to work reprogramming her mind and building up her confidence in both her abilities and herself as a person. At the end of that first session, she left with a huge smile etched on her face.

When she returned to see me the following week, she told me her colleagues had noticed her smile as soon as she walked through the door after our first session. It wasn't long before Danielle flourished. She went on to successfully audition for a part with one of the top ballet companies in the world. Knowing how close she came to quitting, it gave me great pleasure to see her take to the stage and wow audiences with her obvious talent.

What does your inner dialogue say?

If you are struggling with self-esteem and self-confidence issues, a good way to start rebuilding your self-confidence is to cultivate a sense of self-awareness and self-compassion. You can begin by paying attention to any habitual inner dialogue. Many people with low self-confidence and self-esteem have a habit of negative self-talk, which can often be harsh, critical, and self-defeating.

The first step is to recognise and acknowledge these thoughts without judgement. Once you've identified any negative thoughts, you can work on challenging them. Hold each thought up to the light and ask yourself questions like:

- Is this thought true?
- Is there evidence to support this belief?
- Would I say this to a friend or partner?

Answering these questions can help you to see these thoughts more objectively and critically. Treat yourself with the same kindness and understanding you would offer to a friend. Self-compassion involves recognising that everyone makes mistakes and experiences difficulties and challenges. It is OK to be imperfect. Challenging your negative inner thoughts can reduce self-criticism and promote a more supportive inner dialogue.

Time out: reprogramming your inner dialogue

This is a brief hypnosis exercise you can use right now to boost your self-esteem. Make sure you're in a comfortable place, either sitting or lying down, with your eyes closed. Take a couple of nice deep breaths. Inhaling relaxation, exhaling tension.

Imagine an image of yourself now, projected on a screen in front of you. This is your ideal self, with all of the confidence, positive energy and focus that you could possibly want. Let's start now by pressing together your thumb and middle finger, and saying out loud the following affirmations:

→ I am worthy of love and respect.
→ I feel confident in myself.
→ I believe in myself.
→ I am proud of who I am becoming.
→ I am capable of achieving great things.
→ I love and accept myself just as I am.
→ I am strong and resilient.

You can add any additional words of affirmation here, if you feel you need to hear anything else. As you repeat the affirmations, really feel the meaning behind the words. Imagine you're speaking to a loved one, and want them to believe these truths about themselves.

Once you've said your affirmations, two or three times, let your eyes open, returning to the present.

This is a great daily practice to develop, even if you only spend a few minutes on it. The more consistently you do it, the more natural it will feel, and the more effective in boosting your self-esteem it will be.

An optional addition to this practice is to take a moment each day to jot down your thoughts and feelings. As you do so, note any changes in your mood, confidence and attitude over time as you continue the practice.

Writing can be a highly effective tool for improving mental health. It provides an outlet for emotional expression and gives a release. Writing about your thoughts and feelings can help you process emotions, especially challenging, stressful or confusing ones. This can lead to a sense of greater balance, relief and emotional clarity.

Journaling can also serve as a stress management tool. By putting your worries and concerns on paper, you can alleviate some of the mental burden they may create, leading to reduced anxiety and stress levels. Journaling also encourages self-reflection, allowing you to explore your thoughts, feelings and behaviours more deeply, thereby leading to a greater self-awareness and delivering insights into your actions and reactions. You can also track your personal growth over time, reflecting on positive experiences and expressing gratitude.

Writing down positive affirmations, like the ones I shared in the last exercise, can also boost your mood and overall sense of wellbeing.

Other ways to build your self-confidence

Achieving goals can also help you develop your self-confidence by creating a sense of accomplishment. Therefore, set yourself small, realistic goals. Each small task you succeed with will help build your confidence and reinforce a positive self-image.

Affirmations, whether written or spoken, are very important and effective when repeated consistently. Choose affirmations that resonate with you and include them in your daily self-care practice. The key is to repeat them in a comfortable place of clarity. As you do so, you will see a shift in your mindset.

Engaging in hobbies that bring you joy will also improve your self-confidence, as well as boost your mood and dopamine levels. These kinds of activities provide a sense of fulfilment.

Of course, if you are struggling with your self-confidence and it is affecting your life in a negative way, seek support. Hypnotherapy is fantastic at building self-esteem and self-confidence, but this isn't the only option. It is also helpful to talk to a trusted friend or family member. Sharing your feelings and receiving support provides comfort and perspective.

Brenda's story: conquering self-doubt

Having low self-confidence can do more than just affect your mood. For some people, it leads to such high levels of anxiety that they struggle to leave their homes. One of my clients, Brenda, had fallen into just such a negative spiral of low self-confidence.

She was a very bright programmer in her 20s. She seemed to have everything going for her – she was smart, young, attractive – yet she couldn't leave the house. A crisis of self-confidence had struck her. In addition, she was self-medicating with Valium and Xanax, which was contributing to a further downward spiral.

Over the course of five sessions of hypnotherapy, we rebuilt her self-confidence and restored her ability to manage her anxiety. She went from not being able to leave her home to having the confidence to step outside and re-engage with the world. The agoraphobia that had plagued her gradually disappeared. Session by session, I saw her smile returning to her face and could sense her growing confidence.

How self-doubt, fear of failure and imposter syndrome interconnect

In Part 1 we explored both a fear of failure and imposter syndrome and how to begin to overcome them. However, it's important to recognise the crucial role eliminating self-doubt plays in overcoming both a fear of failure and imposter syndrome. When self-doubt feeds into one or both of these things, it creates a vicious cycle of hesitation, uncertainty and insecurity.

I know people who have told me that they believe a bit of self-doubt is helpful, because it creates a platform from which you can strive and work harder. But I disagree with this assessment. When you are using self-doubt to encourage you to work harder, you are like a car running on the wrong type of fuel.

You can't achieve your full potential, and the way in which you're operating is a drain on your energy, time and on your intellectual, physical and emotional resources. By using self-doubt in this way, all you are doing is creating a barrier to having a smoother, happier, more successful and more productive life.

Self-doubt is the enemy of reaching your potential. It's the enemy of enjoying as happy and successful a life as you might otherwise achieve. Hypnosis is very effective at reducing self-doubt, and replacing the self-doubt mindset with a positive expectation of success and confidence.

But it's essential that you recognise when self-doubt has become a negative spiral, and that you can see where it connects to other blocks or challenges you might be experiencing, like a fear of failure or imposter syndrome.

Frank's story: building self-confidence to overcome the imposter within

When Frank first came to see me, he had recently been promoted to the top position in a corporate company. However, he was overcome by a lack of self-confidence and there were signs he was suffering from imposter syndrome.

His lack of self-confidence manifested itself in anxiety, sleepless nights, and repetitive thoughts of changing career and leaving the job for which he'd worked so hard. Each session, I could see a weight lifting from his shoulders and his confidence in himself gradually returning.

We focused on hypnosis and hypnotic suggestions with a powerful dose of confidence to remind him of the reality that he knew deep down – that he was extremely good at his job, well-liked, popular and talented. Over the course of five sessions, we rewired and reprogrammed his subconscious, and the confidence issues that had struck him down dissipated.

Strategies for reducing self-doubt in high-pressure situations

Self-doubt can creep in at the most inconvenient of times, and this is especially true when we are faced with a high-pressure situation. Firstly, it's important to prepare thoroughly for high-pressure situations and interactions. Generally, the more you prepare, the more self-confident and self-assured you'll feel. What's more, practising will further improve your skills and performance.

Positive self-talk is also vital, and hypnosis is fantastic at helping replace negative thoughts with positive affirmations and positive thinking, as we've seen. Breathing is another important tool you can use to help you overcome self-doubt. A simple exercise is to imagine a balloon inflating as you inhale and deflating as you exhale. Focus on breathing into your diaphragm and create an easy flow of breath which oxygenates and further calms your mind and body.

It is also helpful if you can cultivate a success and growth mindset. This means you embrace challenges as opportunities, and see growth in these situations rather than a danger or a threat. A growth mindset can help you view any setbacks as learning experiences, not failures.

Time out: preparing for high-pressure situations

When you are faced with a high-pressure situation and you can feel self-doubt creeping in, take a moment. Press your thumb and middle finger together and mentally repeat the following affirmations:

→ I am able to control adrenaline and anxiety easily and confidently.
→ I believe in myself.
→ I have no self-doubt.

Visualise yourself in the high-pressured situation you are about to face or are preparing for. Perhaps it's an important business pitch to a group of high-powered people who are all watching and listening to you intently. Imagine yourself taking a comfortable breath in and continuing to breathe comfortably. You speak calmly and confidently, fully aware of the information you're expressing. Totally focus on yourself in this visualisation. There is no self-doubt. There's a self-assured energy about you, along with a clarity and freedom from doubt and hesitation.

You can visualise yourself in any situation you need to, all the time focusing on breathing comfortably and feeling calm and in control.

Daniel's story: finding better balance by eliminating self-doubt

One of the challenges with self-doubt is that it can easily become an insidious negative spiral that develops and grows throughout our lives. I remember one of my clients, Daniel, who came to me because he had a major fear of public speaking.

It was even driving him, in his own words, to consider suicide. He had had the problem from the age of eight. He remembered the trauma of the other kids at school laughing at him when he was reading something aloud in class. Ever since, his anxiety, fear and self-doubt had spiralled until it became a consistent nine or ten out of ten.

He was particularly terrified of speaking in a professional context at work, but his self-doubt was having a negative effect on his family life as well as on his career.

When Daniel came to our first session, he looked like a man who was being physically weighed down by the stress and anxiety he felt. An extraordinary thing happened over the course of our sessions together – he physically and mentally transformed in front of my eyes. He told me he felt a calmness that he hadn't experienced in as long as he could remember. Mentally he said he felt a fresh level of positivity and confidence that things were going to be OK in his life. All of this happened as his self-doubt was erased.

When I heard from him a few months later, it was clear he had maintained that same self-confidence, lack of self-doubt and fully embraced a new mindset to not just public speaking, but in managing anxiety in all the areas of his life. This extended to his family life, where previously the dynamics with his wife, their children and his stepchildren had been damaged by his lack of self-confidence, self-doubt and anxiety. Once he had released his self-doubt, Daniel was able to create a positive, confident balance at work, at home and everywhere else in his life.

Assertiveness and self-confidence

Being assertive contributes to both our professional and personal interactions in quite a powerful way. But generally speaking, to behave assertively you need to have a good level of self-confidence. It is a key skill that promotes effective communication, builds stronger relationships, contributes to personal growth and overall wellbeing, and helps you to balance your needs with those of others.

Assertiveness, like self-confidence, is important in a professional context because it demonstrates that you have the ability to handle conflicts constructively. Instead of avoiding issues, when you are assertive you can address problems directly and collaboratively, which leads to more effective resolutions.

In your personal life, assertiveness helps to resolve disagreements with family members, friends and loved ones, and reduces the possibility of conflict escalating. In short, it's an important part of being clear in your communication. Being assertive can help you clearly and openly express your own thoughts, desires, needs and expectations, reducing misunderstandings in the process. All of this creates greater transparency and strengthens bonds, on a personal and professional level.

When you demonstrate assertive behaviour in the workplace, you not only show self-respect, but also respect for others by being able to stand up for your ideas while being open to others' viewpoints. Assertiveness creates a culture of mutual respect in workplaces, and shows that you value what others have to say. This behaviour also has a similar effect in our private lives, creating more balanced and respectful relationships across the board.

Assertiveness is closely tied to self-esteem and self-confidence, because when you assert yourself, you affirm your values, abilities and boundaries. This is like a positive feedback loop, because each time you are assertive, it boosts your self-confidence and self-belief. In a work context, this often leads to far greater job satisfaction, as well as promotions and career advancement.

In your personal relationships, assertiveness helps you to maintain a positive self-image by ensuring your needs are met and that you are treated with real respect. Assertiveness also helps with effective decision-making. When you understand and communicate your own goals, objectives and values, whilst being open to others' input, you are more likely to make more informed and confident decisions.

Assertiveness also can reduce stress. When you set boundaries and communicate them clearly, you are less likely to take on too much work. You also remove stress by voicing complaints, frustrations and resentments in a respectful way, rather than allowing them to fester in your mind.

Being assertive helps you manage your time and energy better in every area of your life, because by setting boundaries you avoid over-commitment. This often leads to a healthier, more balanced life. It also fosters open communication, leading to better teamwork and collaboration in the workplace, while building trust. When you are assertive, you can navigate various social dynamics with confidence, openness and respect.

Diana's story: escaping from controlling behaviour

Diana's lack of assertiveness in her personal relationship was taking a serious toll on her mental health. She allowed her partner to dictate, influence and control her life. He showed signs of controlling and coercive behaviour, which Diana had let go unchecked for years.

Session by session, I could see the hypnosis was having a powerful effect on Diana. She was developing a new way of thinking. She had a new-found confidence and it was clear she would no longer put up with her partner's controlling behaviour.

Diana started the process of taking back control by having an open, honest and boundaried conversation with her partner, where she set out the behaviour that he needed to change and gave a timescale during which things needed to change. To her partner's credit, he reflected and recognised that he needed to change his behaviour and, he did.

However, Diana continued to become more confident and was consistently more assertive in their relationship. Some weeks after our final session, she told me that she had taken the decision to end their ten-year relationship, and that she was happier, felt clear-headed and knew it was the right decision for both of them.

She was amazed by how the hypnosis had helped her develop the strength to no longer put up with controlling, abusive, unwanted and unhealthy behaviours, and to assert her views. She also told me that this was having a positive knock-on effect at work, where she was feeling more comfortable talking to her boss about balancing her time, and ensuring she did not become overloaded with projects.

Fear: the challenge to being assertive

Fear is one of the greatest challenges to our ability to be assertive. Most commonly, a fear of conflict or fear of rejection will hold us back from being assertive. A fear of what others will think of us or fear of hurting other people's feelings can also prevent us from being more assertive.

However, this is a largely irrational fear that stems from low self-confidence and self-esteem. When we doubt our own worth it is easy to fear that our opinions are not valuable enough to be heard, which prevents us from asserting ourselves in a healthy way.

Another common side-effect of being afraid to be assertive is that we struggle to say no, leading to overcommitment and in some cases burnout. Our fear of disappointing others often drives this behaviour. For some people, there can also be socio-cultural norms that discourage assertiveness.

It's important to point out here that assertiveness does not mean you are aggressive – although many people conflate the two words. Again this can prevent you from being assertive because you fear being seen as too forceful or demanding. The truth is that assertiveness is all about communicating our needs effectively and setting clear boundaries.

If you habitually avoid being assertive to avoid conflict, then it is likely that you will also be struggling to set boundaries that protect you, and to openly share your needs and desires. Strong emotions, like anger or anxiety, can make it more challenging to remain calm and assertive. Therefore, we need to be mindful of how we are feeling in any given situation and find techniques that can bring us back to a calm state to enable us to have these conversations in a constructive manner.

Flex your assertiveness muscle

Developing assertiveness is a gradual process. Just like everything else it requires practice, repetition, reinforcement and self-reflection. An important first step is understanding exactly what assertiveness is. Recognising that assertiveness is the ability to express your thoughts and feelings or needs directly, openly and honestly, whilst also respecting the rights and feelings of others can make it feel less "scary".

Take some time now to evaluate how you currently communicate. Do you tend to be passive in exchanges, or aggressive? What might you need to do to come across as assertive?

There is no single way to be more assertive, as this will change depending on the situation, so make sure you also take time to reflect on what you need and want in different situations. Knowing what your goals and priorities are helps you to communicate them much more effectively.

Recognise that you have the right, like anyone else, to express your needs, say no and set boundaries without feeling any guilt.

Use "I" statements in your communication to make it clear, and ensure you are being direct and specific when you state your needs or concerns. You have to move away from being vague or hinting. Make sure you maintain a calm and steady voice while you are talking. Try using phrases like the following:

- I feel overwhelmed.
- I feel unappreciated in this relationship.

Think about how much better those sound than saying, "You give me too much work", or "You don't appreciate me".

> **Time out: affirmations for assertiveness**
>
> Take a moment to practise being more assertive right now. Make sure you are in a comfortable, safe space and close your eyes. Bring your thumb and middle finger to touch on each hand. Take two nice deep breaths, and repeat the following affirmations to yourself:
>
> → I respect my own boundaries.
> → I enforce my own boundaries.
> → I feel comfortable explaining that I can't take on another project right now in the workplace.
> → I am comfortable asserting my feelings, my desires and my needs on a daily basis.
> → I set boundaries without feeling guilty.
> → I have the right to express my needs.
>
> Once you have said each of those affirmations at least twice, let your eyes open and continue with your day.

Consistency is the key to not only becoming more assertive, but also to forming good habits and creating new neural connections in the brain. There are many small shifts we can make to our behaviour to enforce assertiveness respectfully.

Making and maintaining eye contact shows confidence and attentiveness, so make eye contact as much as you can without staring. Good posture conveys confidence, so avoid slouching or crossing your arms, which can signal defensiveness or insecurity. Make open gestures with your hands to emphasise the points you are making, and avoid pointing or aggressive gestures. Keep your body language open. And remember that assertiveness is a skill which, like all skills, improves with consistent practice.

Chapter Five

Breaking the Cycle of Addiction and Bad Habits

Breaking free from addictive patterns is often a very challenging experience and I see clients with various addiction issues on virtually a daily basis in my clinic. To free yourself from addictive patterns requires commitment, self-awareness and often positive support from others.

First and foremost though, you need to admit you have an addiction problem and then seek out the various interventions and solutions that are most likely to work for you. Obviously I'm a big advocate of hypnosis and hypnotherapy. The key to any therapy succeeding, however, is recognising and accepting you have an addictive pattern of behaviour.

As I've said already in this book, for hypnosis to work there needs to be a strong desire for change. So, if you have realised you have an addiction problem, take some time to reflect on how it's impacting your life emotionally, physically, socially and financially. Journaling can be a useful tool for this kind of self-reflection, or you may find talking with trusted friends or reaching out to a therapist or a hypnotherapist is a suitable course of action for you.

During your reflections, it is important to identify the triggers for your addiction. In doing so you will come to understand what leads to your addictive behaviour. Your trigger might be stress, boredom, certain social situations or a specific emotional state, like loneliness or anger. It can be helpful to keep a log of when and why you engage in addictive behaviour, because noticing patterns can help you anticipate and avoid triggers.

When it comes to breaking free from addiction, this will look different for each of us. However, it is important to set clear goals for what this looks like *for you* at the start of this process. Does it mean complete abstinence? Do you merely want to reduce a specific behaviour? Or are you looking to control and moderate your behaviour? Whichever way you choose to tackle your addiction, hypnosis can help reset your mind and give you control.

As well as setting goals, it is important to develop a structured plan that shows you how you will achieve your goals. This plan should include strategies for avoiding triggers, as well as refer to any positive habits that you want to replace your addiction with.

Hypnosis can be particularly beneficial here because it can rewire your brain so that your triggers are no longer triggers. It is also very helpful for replacing an addiction with positive habits. Having healthier activities or habits to replace your addiction reduces temptation and, therefore, the chances of a relapse.

Through hypnosis, you can build resilience, increase your positive willpower and strengthen your ability to cope with any kind of craving or setback on your journey.

I find it is important that you focus on the present when you are tackling an addiction. Monitoring your progress so that you can assess how well you're sticking to your new habits often gives you momentum to keep going, but this is also a chance to check in on how you feel without your addiction. What positive changes have you seen in your life as a result of breaking free of your addiction?

Understanding the addiction cycle

There are powerful psychochemical components to addiction that can make it very difficult to overcome, even if the person in question is able to rationally understand how damaging their addiction is for their lives. Addiction doesn't happen overnight, especially if we're talking about substance addiction. It is a chronic brain disease that affects the brain's reward system where the dopamine, pleasure, memory, motivation and reward centres are all located.

As with any other chronic illness, there are a series of stages that addicts go through. It can take weeks, months or even years for an addiction to fully develop. The following stages are the broad cycle of an addiction, but some of these stages may occur simultaneously. It's not a wholly linear process.

1. **Initial use:** This is when you first use an addictive substance. An initial use doesn't necessarily lead to addiction, but without it a pattern of addiction can't occur. This could be something as seemingly benign as taking a strong painkiller offered by a friend, or it might be your first cigarette or alcoholic drink.

2. **Abuse:** This is when the addiction cycle truly kicks in. It is when an individual starts using the substance on a recurring and improper basis in a harmful way.

3. **Tolerance:** At this stage, the substance can cause changes in the brain that result in tolerance. This is a condition described by Merck's manuals (medical references published by the America pharmaceutical company Merck & Co) as one in which the original dose no longer produces the same physical or mental effects, so the dosage typically increases in frequency.

4. **Dependence:** Now the body or brain becomes dependent on having the substance to be able to function properly. As an example, a person who has been using cocaine for a long time may find it impossible to feel pleasure without the drug.

5. **Addiction:** This is when defined symptoms can be used to diagnose addiction as a condition and result in a related set of issues.

6. **Relapse:** At this point, an addict knows that the substance is damaging for them and often destructive or deadly, but they just cannot break that cycle. Their addiction becomes a cycle of self-harm. It is such a strong habit and they often feel such a powerful compulsion that they're in the casino gambling, lighting up a cigarette, snorting a line of cocaine, calling their drug dealer, or opening that third bottle of wine before they really know that they are doing it. Their subconscious urge for whatever substance they are addicted to is so powerful it takes over.

Gavin's story: breaking the self-destructive cycle

Gavin was a ketamine addict of seven years when I started treating him. He was in a very sorry state. His dad even accompanied him to our first session, where he told me that he had lost his son. Gavin was married with a two-year-old daughter and he had a good job. He had a family who loved him. But despite all of these

Part Two: Regaining Control and Breaking Bad Cycles

very compelling, rational reasons to get clean, all he could think about was ketamine.

How he would score some and when he could have his next hit consumed every waking moment for him. His wife gave him one final chance to get clean. He was continually receiving warnings at work. He had been hospitalised three times within the previous 12 months and been told that the drug was slowly eating away his insides.

In our first session, Gavin told me that he knew ketamine was ruining his life, but also that it was all he could think about from the moment he woke up.

There was no clear trigger for Gavin. In his case, he had become so used to the psychological high he got from the drug that he didn't think he could live without it. It was clear to me that our hypnosis needed to work if we were to save his life, and bring peace to his loved ones.

We had 12 sessions together, and during that period there were highs and lows. Gavin experienced relapses but, by the end of our sessions, he was completely clean and off the ketamine. He changed jobs and rebuilt his relationships with his family and friends.

His wife called me, shedding tears of happiness as she shared her appreciation for how our sessions had turned Gavin's life around. She said our work had made them into a family again, with a future to look forward to.

Getting to know your triggers

Understanding the triggers for your addictive behaviours, or bad habits, is crucial in terms of prevention and treatment. When you can recognise what triggers your addictive behaviour or bad habit, you can take proactive steps to avoid or manage those triggers before they lead to harm.

For example, perhaps experiencing stress and anxiety is a trigger for smoking or drinking. In which case, you can focus on reducing and managing your anxiety and stress to prevent that habit from developing or worsening.

When you know what your triggers are, it can also help you identify high-risk situations or environments. This is crucial whether you are preventing an addiction or habit from developing further, or want to avoid a relapse.

Addictive behaviours and bad habits are often coping mechanisms for underlying emotional or psychological issues, such as anxiety, depression or trauma. In other cases, an addiction or bad habit is created in the neurocircuitry of the brain and is a result of the chemical dopamine and its relationship to the habit or addiction.

Whatever kind of addictive behaviour or bad habit you are trying to break, it is crucial that you understand that you have a problem. You also need to have a willingness to be open and seek help.

This openness and willingness is particularly critical for the success of hypnotherapy. When you recognise the need to change, it is much easier for hypnosis to rewire a new mindset which effectively neutralises your triggers. When hypnosis is effective, you won't react to a trigger when you encounter it, because in your mind, this is no longer a trigger for a specific pattern of behaviour. This might sound too good to be true, but I promise that I have seen it time and again in my work with addicts.

Removing the trigger for the addiction or bad habit can lead to incredible improvements in every aspect of your life, from your physical health, relationships and work performance, to your wellbeing and happiness levels.

Chloe's story: identifying the trauma behind the addiction

I first met Chloe when she was 28. She had been through heroin addiction and was on methadone. She came to me because she was seeking therapy to come off the drugs completely. Of course, before we started a course of hypnotherapy, I spoke to her other doctors and therapists to ensure that it was safe for her to withdraw from the methadone in a controlled way.

For the hypnosis to be most effective, I felt it was important that we identified the trigger for Chloe's addiction. This led us to the lack of love she had experienced as a child, which was the main trauma that encouraged her to turn to drugs to feel a sense of total escape and love. Through the heroin, and then the methadone, Chloe was able to create her own bubble of love, protection and carefree release – feelings that had been sadly lacking in her childhood.

Therefore, the focus of our hypnotherapy sessions was for her to feel that self-love, protection, safety and trust without having to take any drug to get there. The hypnotherapy worked beautifully, and Chloe was able to completely come off the methadone.

Once she was clean, she was able to fulfil her potential and she turned her life around. During our first session, Chloe told me that she wanted to write, produce and perform music. By the time our six sessions had finished, she was indeed writing, producing and performing music. It was wonderful to see how she transformed her life.

Recognising how addictions can be interlinked

In some cases, multiple addictions can interlink. One that I have seen several times during my years of practising hypnotherapy is a crystal meth addiction combined with a sex addiction. Crystal meth is a powerful stimulant that significantly increases dopamine levels in the brain. Dopamine is a neurotransmitter associated with pleasure, reward and motivation, which means the surge in dopamine from crystal meth use produces intense euphoria and heightened arousal. This is linked to an increased desire for sex.

Chemsex – the term used when someone combines drug use with sex – often involves marathon sexual sessions that can last for many hours or even days. The intense pleasure and euphoria associated with this combination reinforces this powerfully addictive behaviour.

However, the combination of crystal meth use and sex addiction often leads to severe psychological issues, such as anxiety, depression, paranoia and psychosis. Anxiety, malnutrition and social isolation often come hand in hand with these issues. What's more, crystal meth use leads to long-term changes in the brain's reward system, particularly in areas like the nucleus, lumbar and prefrontal cortex. These changes can result in increased impulsivity and a diminished capacity to experience pleasure from natural rewards, such as normal sexual activity without the drug use.

For treatment and hypnotherapy to be effective in such cases, we need to address the chemical dependency on crystal meth alongside the behavioural aspects of the sex addiction. The individual also has to be fully engaged in the process and want to break their addictive pattern of behaviour. When they are, they can be free of both addictions within just seven hypnotherapy sessions.

Stephen's story: breaking free of a double addiction

One of my more surprising clients was an 85 year old man, Stephen, who became addicted to crack-cocaine around the age of 82 or 83, which is unusually late in life. But in addition to his drug addiction, he used to engage in gay sex while taking crack cocaine. He would disappear from his family home and leave his wife around once a month, sometimes more, to go on crack-cocaine and sex benders lasting 10–12 hours at a time.

At his age, it was a miracle that his body survived the drugs and long sex sessions. Stephen underwent a series of hypnotherapy sessions with me to break both addictions. Fortunately, the hypnosis worked and probably saved his life, as none of us were sure how much longer his body would have been able to withstand his behaviour.

Replacing destructive behaviours with healthy habits

When you replace destructive behaviours with healthy habits, you are not only doing so to break the destructive cycle of behaviour you've fallen into, but are also improving your wellbeing over the long term, contributing to your personal growth and bringing more happiness into your life.

The challenge for many of us is that simply stopping bad behaviours without replacing them with healthier alternatives can leave a void and increase the likelihood of a relapse. Healthy habits serve the dual purpose of providing a positive way to cope with stresses and reducing the risk of returning to any destructive behaviour.

Consistency is the key to creating healthy habits. If you want to try daily hypnosis, my app *Subconsciously* provides a daily practice that can reinforce a new, more positive mindset. It is also advisable to introduce regular physical activity into your life, as well as regular social engagements. Both these things can help manage stress and anxiety, as well as improve your mood.

Engaging in healthy habits creates a platform for continued long-term recovery and personal development, as well as building your confidence and fostering a sense of accomplishment and self-worth. As individuals replace destructive behaviours with positive ones, with the help of hypnosis or other mental health interventions, they build confidence in their ability to make positive changes, further strengthening that subconscious commitment to long-term success.

Healthy habits also contribute to the development of a positive self-identity. This helps you move away from identifying as someone who engages in destructive behaviour, which in turn becomes a self-fulfilling prophecy. The more you engage in healthy habits, the more you will see yourself as someone who makes the right, healthy and constructive choices. This further reinforces recovery and growth.

The power of healthy habits

Habits are formed through repeated behaviours that create neural pathways in the brain. Destructive behaviour reinforces negative neural pathways, while healthy habits can help establish new positive pathways. Over time, these healthier pathways become stronger, making the positive behaviour more automatic, and reducing any kind of gravitation to old destructive habits.

Neuroplasticity, which is the brain's ability to change and adapt, allows us to replace negative habits with positive ones. This leads to lasting changes in brain function and spawns long-term behavioural change that supports recovery.

Healthy habits also contribute to a more balanced and satisfying life. Engaging in habits like exercise, meaningful social interactions, hobbies and self-care not only helps you to avoid destructive behaviours, but also adds a sense of joy, focus, purpose, peace and fulfilment to your daily life. As destructive behaviours often strain relationships with family, friends, colleagues and intimate partners, replacing these behaviours with healthy habits can also repair and strengthen relationships. This results in more supportive and fulfilling social networks.

Destructive behaviours can also derail personal and professional goals, by consuming our time, energy and resources, not to mention in some cases causing us to behave badly. When you replace these destructive behaviours with healthy habits, you can more easily focus on your goals and aspirations, leading to a greater sense of satisfaction in life.

Healthy habits create a foundation for sustainable long-term change. By consistently engaging in positive behaviours, this new momentum supports ongoing personal growth and achievement. As I've mentioned, many destructive behaviours are used as maladaptive coping mechanisms for anxiety or trauma. Replacing these with healthy habits like hypnosis, meditation or physical activity creates positive outlooks that are creative outlets for more effective and sustainable ways to reduce anxiety, or stress, without harmful consequences.

Healthy habits also help build resilience, enabling you to handle life's challenges more effectively. Resilience is crucial for maintaining your recovery and avoiding returning to destructive behaviours. The rewards of healthy habits such as feeling more energetic, achieving personal goals and enjoying stronger and more meaningful relationships, also provide ongoing motivation to maintain and increase these positive behaviours. This also makes a relapse into destructive habits less and less likely.

Suggestions for healthy habit swaps

There are many healthy habits that you can swap for destructive and damaging behaviours. The key is to find a habit (or habits) that works for you. They need to be something you enjoy, otherwise you won't maintain the consistency you need to turn them into habits. To give you some ideas, I've shared some of the most common healthy habit swaps out there, but this is not an exhaustive list. Think about what will work for you.

- Smoking is often associated with stress relief and taking breaks, so swap this for deep breathing exercises. They can provide similar relaxation benefits, reduce stress and lower anxiety. Simply breathe in deeply through your nose, hold the breath for a few seconds, and then exhale slowly through your mouth. Repeat this whenever you feel you need to unwind, and especially whenever you feel the urge to smoke.
- For some smokers, the oral sensation of having a cigarette in their mouth is important. If this is something you identify with, try swapping cigarettes for sugar-free gum.
- Many people drink alcohol in social situations, and a simple swap is to find a non-alcoholic drink that you can opt for instead. That might be a zero-alcohol beer, or it could be fruit juice or even herbal tea. Find a soothing, satisfying alternative that suits your tastes. If you always drink alcohol at certain times of day, create a new ritual with your favourite non-alcoholic drink. Focus on what you are drinking and make sure you enjoy it.

- Physical activity is a natural mood booster because it releases endorphins. Work out where you can incorporate physical exercise into your routine, whether that is walking, jogging, swimming or attending a class at the gym. This can be a great habit if you notice that stress relief or boredom is your trigger for your addictive behaviour.
- Mindful eating is great if your addictive behaviour is eating or food related. Mindful eating makes you more aware of when you're actually hungry – and, therefore, when you need to eat – as well as helping you recognise when you have satisfied that hunger. Focus on enjoying the taste of your food. Savour each bite and pay attention to the textures, flavours and smell of your food. Avoid distractions like TV or your phone while you're eating so you can really concentrate on your meal.
- Replace unhealthy snacks with healthy alternatives, like pre-cut vegetables or fruit. Often it is the ease and convenience of unhealthy foods that makes us reach for them. Plan ahead make sure you have some pre-cut fruit or vegetables available for whenever you get a craving.
- Identify hobbies that interest you, and fill your time with those instead of unhealthy or unhelpful habits, like scrolling on social media. Perhaps you want to read more books, get into gardening, start painting, learn a musical instrument or pick up a new language. Set aside a specific time for this activity or hobby to help it become part of your life.
- Set screen time limits if you are addicted to your phone or social media. Establish certain times of the day during which you disconnect from your device. You might use an app to track your screen time. One of the most effective ways to break this addiction is to replace online activities with offline ones. Spend time outdoors with your loved ones rather than mindlessly scrolling on social media, for instance.

- Volunteering is a great and very positive alternative to engaging in unhelpful or damaging habits. Helping others can provide a sense of purpose and fulfilment, and give you a positive focus to replace the likes of the temporary high of drug use. Find a local organisation or cause that resonates with you and volunteer your time to contribute positively to your community and broader society.
- Engaging in creative activities like arts, music, or writing, can be a powerful way to express your emotions and deal with other underlying stresses, anxieties or traumas, or even just boredom. Each time you feel yourself leaning towards an old, bad habit, try doing something creative instead and see what happens.
- Hypnosis and hypnotherapy can be incredibly valuable to help you overcome addiction and build new, positive habits to prevent a relapse.

Finding healthy alternatives to replace destructive behaviours or bad habits can significantly contribute to you having a happier and more fulfilling life. Some of the healthy activities I've suggested here, like regular exercise and eating a balanced diet, will boost your physical health, leading to increased energy and vitality. This can make your daily activities easier and more enjoyable, contributing to a greater sense of wellbeing, fulfilment and happiness.

Adopting these healthy habits also lowers your risk of chronic conditions such as heart disease, diabetes and obesity. Meanwhile a healthier body supports a more active and fulfilling lifestyle, allowing you to engage more fully in life's opportunities.

Healthy habits also support the pursuit and achievement of your long-term goals, whether these relate to your career, personal development or relationships. Maintaining healthy alternatives helps you stay focused, motivated and shows you that you are capable of overcoming obstacles.

Time out: adopt one new healthy habit

I would encourage you to take up one or more of the healthy alternatives I've outlined in this chapter. Choose one that appeals to you and introduce it to your life once a week.

Once you are consistently doing it, gradually increase the frequency. Write down the positive rewards you get from engaging with that healthy alternative, in your diary. If it's going well, choose another healthy habit and introduce that to your life in the same way.

My top tip to help you stay on track is to keep a journal of your progress where you make a daily or weekly note of:

→ Positive changes you notice.
→ Your progression.
→ Your happiness.
→ Changes in your mood.
→ Your healthy habit streaks.
→ Any personal goals you achieve along the way.

Each week or month, look back at what you've recorded. Can you see improvements in your happiness and wellbeing? Are you building resilience? How much more have you achieved by focusing on one or more healthy habits rather than your unhealthy, damaging or addictive behaviours?

Remember that healthy doesn't have to mean boring, time-consuming, off-putting or unpleasurable. Most of the time, this combination of hobbies, exercise and changing habits around eating can actually be more pleasurable, more enjoyable and give you greater levels of calmness, dopamine production and serotonin production than you had with your unhealthy behaviour.

What's more, healthy habits deliver this in a happier, healthier, more sustainable way. You'll experience fewer peaks and troughs, more balance, more pleasure, more sense of achievement, more sense of peace, more sense of positivity, more sense of contentment and a greater sense that you are moving towards fulfilling your potential.

Chapter Six

Stopping Procrastination

Procrastination can become an ingrained habit pattern and it's one that can have an impact on more than you might imagine. In fact, procrastination negatively impacts so much in life – it stops us from being as happy, fulfilled or successful as we otherwise might be. It can also lead to a low level of satisfaction with our lives and cause low moods, depression and anxiety.

One study conducted by Sirois, Stride and Pychyl found that chronic procrastination is strongly associated with stress.[13] This often has negative health implications as those who procrastinate are subjected to higher levels of stress over prolonged periods of time. In addition, research conducted by Flett, Haghbin and Pychyl found that procrastinators are

---

13   Sirois, F.M., Stride, C.B. and Pychyl, T.A. (2023) 'Procrastination and health: A longitudinal test of the roles of stress and health behaviours,' *British Journal of Health Psychology*, 28(3), pp. 860–875. https://doi.org/10.1111/bjhp.12658.

likely to be more vulnerable to suffering from depression than those who don't procrastinate.[14]

There are numerous other pieces of research that indicate that procrastination contributes to depressive symptoms, increases feelings of guilt, shame and hopelessness, decreases self-esteem and leads to lower levels of life satisfaction. A further study by Sirois and Pychyl found that procrastinators often struggle to regulate their emotions, which can lead to avoidant behaviours and increased procrastination.[15]

So, while procrastination is not strictly considered a mental health condition, it is connected to many mental health challenges. Fear is a powerful reason why many of us procrastinate. The fear of failing, as we've discussed, can be a powerful driver of unhelpful behaviour. Fear of falling into the fear cycle itself can also lead to procrastination.

So what happens when we stop procrastinating? We unblock what's been stuck in our lives, enter a state of flow, and experience a vastly different level of satisfaction, contentment and joy in life. Of course, we'll also experience a simple improvement in our day-to-day productivity, cohesion, pleasure, and an overall fluidity and positive momentum in our lives. All of this helps put you in a positive mood and can help you cultivate a more positive outlook on life.

---

14 Flett, A. L., Haghbin, M., & Pychyl, T. A. (2016). Procrastination and depression from a cognitive perspective: An exploration of the associations among procrastinatory automatic thoughts, rumination, and mindfulness. Journal of Rational-Emotive & Cognitive-Behavior Therapy, 34(3), 169–186. https://doi.org/10.1007/s10942-016-0235-1

15 Pychyl, T. A., & Sirois, F. M. (2016). Procrastination, emotion regulation, and well-being. In F. M. Sirois & T. A. Pychyl (Eds.), Procrastination, health, and well-being (pp. 163–188). Elsevier Academic Press. https://doi.org/10.1016/B978-0-12-802862-9.00008-6

Petra's story: finding the courage to make a change

I remember one of my clients, Petra, who came to me because she had some brilliant ideas for creating her own fashion brand. However, she couldn't find it within herself to leave the corporate fashion world, where she worked at that time. She knew she couldn't develop her business idea while in her full-time job, but fear was making her procrastinate about taking the leap.

The hypnotherapy worked a treat and unlocked the "I will, I can, I'm doing it…" spirit within her. Over the course of five sessions, we unlocked the action-taking side of Petra's personality and this encouraged her to take the bull by the horns. She seized the opportunity in front of her. A few months after our sessions, she contacted me to say that she'd set up her own business and that it was going really well.

But getting over procrastination changed Petra in many ways – she experienced improvements mentally, financially, in her relationships with others and in her mood.

Why do we procrastinate?

Procrastination is a highly complex behaviour that is influenced by a variety of psychological and emotional factors. However, the overriding driver of procrastination is fear – a fear of failure or fear of not meeting expectations are among the most common.

This kind of fear often stems from perfectionism or a belief that your self-worth is tied to results and performance. When this fear takes hold, you tend to put off tasks, especially those that have higher stakes. Instead, you focus on less important, lower priority tasks. This gives you a sense that you are doing something, but often results in a lack of significant progress. It can be easy for this to become a long-term habit pattern.

Perfectionists in particular often procrastinate because they set unrealistically high bars for themselves. The thought of not being able to achieve those standards often leads to avoidance. That means you delay starting tasks because you feel you don't have enough time to do it perfectly, or that you are not ready yet.

Low self-efficacy is another reason we procrastinate. This refers to concerns over our ability to complete tasks successfully, which means we are more likely to procrastinate. Low self-efficacy is often tied to past experiences of failure or a lack of confidence in certain skills and abilities. Therefore, you might avoid tasks that you perceive as difficult or outside your comfort zone. This often leads to a cycle of procrastination which further damages your self-confidence and self-belief.

What does this look like in reality? Let's imagine you need to start a challenging, complex project. Every time you attempt to start the project, you might find yourself surfing the internet, cleaning up or even emotionally eating, which is very common amongst my clients.

Another factor that can lead to procrastination is a concept known as temporal discounting. This is when we value immediate rewards more than future ones. As a result, we procrastinate over tasks that will deliver a delayed benefit in favour of doing tasks that bring immediate gratification. So, you might decide to go out for a meal with friends or even just surf the net rather than working on a long-term project, even though you know that putting off the project work will lead to stress later on.

Task aversion is another reason why we may procrastinate. This is when we see a task as unpleasant, boring or overwhelming and because of our aversion to that task we avoid it, leading to a negative cycle of procrastination. That means we might delay important tasks, like filing our taxes, because we find it tedious or boring, and instead favour activities that give us an immediate dopamine hit.

A lack of motivation can often lead to procrastination too. Motivation can be affected by factors such as interest in the task and the perceived value and relevance of the task to our personal goals. The less motivated we are to do something, the more likely we are to procrastinate. Low motivation often occurs when a task doesn't align with our values or interests.

So, you might postpone a work assignment because it doesn't seem meaningful or connected to your career aspirations, even though this procrastination results in last-minute stress.

Decision fatigue is another important factor that causes procrastination When faced with too many choices or decisions, we can experience decision fatigue leading to procrastination. It's a way to avoid the mental effort of making a choice. You might delay starting a project because you're overwhelmed by the number of decisions you need to make, such as how to organise your work or which tasks to prioritise. I often see this happening to my clients.

Distraction and the lack of focus is yet another driver of procrastination. In a world filled with distraction, it's easy to lose focus on the task at hand. Constant interruptions can lead to procrastination as tasks tend to take longer to complete. You might find yourself frequently checking your phone, social media or emails instead of focusing on the task, again leading to this compounding of delays in completing your work and the vicious cycle continues.

Another key factor behind procrastination, based on what I see in my practice, is difficulties regulating emotions. Procrastination can be a way to avoid negative emotions such as anxiety or boredom. Therefore, you might delay tasks to temporarily avoid these feelings even if it leads to more stress later. For example, you may put off having a difficult conversation or addressing a problem because it feels too emotionally taxing, even though you know it needs to be done.

Finally, your self-identity can be another reason why you procrastinate. More specifically, when you struggle with your self-identity or how you see yourself in relation to the task, you are more likely to avoid it. For example, if you see yourself as a creative person, but have to do a highly analytical task, you might delay it because it doesn't align with your self-identity.

The problem is that, whatever the reason behind your procrastination, all it does is perpetuate the vicious cycle that you're in. Therefore, recognising the underlying psychological causes of procrastination can help in developing solutions and strategies that will overcome it. Whatever the reason behind your procrastination, hypnotherapy can help because it is fantastic at rewiring our brains, identifying the issue and reprogramming it.

Ahmed's story: breaking out of the procrastination cycle

Ahmed had a number of brilliant social media marketing AI concepts, along with various other business projects. He was a very talented guy, but one who procrastinated chronically. This was partly due to a fear of failing and partly due to a fear of succeeding. His procrastination exacerbated his anxiety and low mood, which fed into a cycle of negative self-talk and almost a version of self-harming.

Through around eight sessions, we built up Ahmed's confidence and I saw his procrastination lessen. By the end of our sessions, his mood had improved so much that all his procrastinating behaviour had stopped. He was on a high, likely due to the dopamine hits and impact of the serotonin his body produced when he ticked tasks off his list and saw not only the financial rewards of doing so, but also the happy customers.

It was a joy to see Ahmed's business vision coming to life before his eyes. Alongside his professional success, he also saw improvements in his personal life as he achieved better balance, a new perspective, a greater sense of proportion, and improved health both mentally and physically.

The key to successfully overcoming procrastination in Ahmed's case, as it is for many of my clients, is their desire to change, to grow and to break the cycle of procrastination. Remember that people of all backgrounds and abilities are affected by procrastination. You can be incredibly successful and still procrastinate to the point that it negatively impacts your life. But if you truly want to change, you will make time in your day to use tools like hypnosis to help you overcome and break free of your negative cycle of procrastination.

The value of time management strategies when tackling procrastination

While hypnosis is incredibly effective at helping you break the cycle of procrastination, it is also important to develop effective time management techniques to not only break that cycle, but to maintain a more positive habit pattern.

In essence, you want to address the underlying causes of your procrastination and then use these techniques to create a structured environment that encourages productivity. As we've discussed, feelings of overwhelm are common among those who procrastinate. This is why task prioritisation and breaking large tasks down into smaller, more manageable steps, can be so useful for overcoming the overwhelm and, therefore, the procrastination.

Here are some simple techniques you can try to help you overcome your procrastination:

- **Chunking:** This is the process of grouping different bits of information together into more manageable chunks. In doing so, you make information clearer and easier to remember for yourself and others. Your mind also naturally divides large pieces of information into smaller units.
- **Create clear deadlines:** Without clear deadlines tasks can feel open-ended, leading to a lack of urgency and increased procrastination. Setting specific deadlines for tasks, even self-imposed ones, creates a sense of urgency and helps you prioritise those tasks.
- **The Pomodoro technique:** This is where you work in short and timed intervals, which can help create a rhythm that makes it easier to stay on track.
- **The Eisenhower Matrix:** Prioritising tasks is key. When faced with multiple tasks, many of us procrastinate because we are unsure which task to start with or because we avoid the most important ones. Techniques like the Eisenhower Matrix, where you categorise tasks by urgency and importance, help identify which tasks should be tackled first. Urgent and important tasks are those that require immediate attention and are critical to achieving your goals. Tasks that are not urgent, but important, are essential for your long-term success, but do not require immediate action. The urgent, but not important, tasks might need attention, but do not contribute to your long-term goals. Of course, the tasks that are not urgent and not important are the first that you should cut out because they do not contribute significantly to what you're trying to achieve. By

focusing on high-priority (important) tasks, you can avoid procrastinating on important work.
- **Reduce decision fatigue:** Constantly making decisions about what to do next can be exhausting, leading to procrastination as a way to avoid making those decisions. Planning ahead and creating a daily or weekly schedule can reduce decision fatigue by providing a clear roadmap of what needs to be done and when. This allows you to focus on execution rather than decision making.
- **Just start:** It's important to build momentum and starting a task is often the hardest part. Procrastination thrives in the absence of momentum, so creating momentum is one of the hypnotic suggestions that I use when I'm supporting clients who have procrastination issues. Seeing clients rewiring their mindset to create momentum and a positive flow that reinforces a sense of satisfaction, pleasure, achievement and accomplishment is a common part of my work.
- **Time-blocking:** This is where you dedicate specific time slots to specific tasks. Often starting with easier tasks on your list can help build momentum. Once you start working and achieve small wins, it becomes easier to continue working on more challenging tasks.
- **Improve focus and minimise distractions:** Distractions and lack of focus are major contributors to procrastination. Create a distraction-free environment by doing things like disabling desktop notifications on your computer and putting your phone in another room.
- **Visualise ticking your tasks off your list:** I often get my clients to visualise themselves ticking tasks off their list, one at a time, and encourage them to enjoy the sense of satisfaction this brings. This can help give them the momentum they need to get started on their important tasks.
- **Use a to-do list:** A list helps keep your mind focused on what needs to be done.

- **Set yourself goals and rewards:** This can help enhance your motivation to tackle a specific task and create a positive cycle of activity. By breaking tasks into smaller steps, with rewards along the way, you further create a positive feedback loop that encourages continued progress.
- **Manage stress and anxiety:** Stress and anxiety about a task leads to procrastination. Reduce these feelings as much as possible by organising both your tasks and your time using some of the techniques I've shared here. When you know what needs to be done and have a plan in place, you can approach tasks with a much clearer, more relaxed mindset.
- **Establish a routine:** A lack of structure and consistency can lead to procrastination. It is much easier to put tasks off without a clear routine, so make sure you have a routine for each day and stay consistent. This will create a sense of order and predictability, as well as quell any feelings of stress or anxiety. Schedule certain tasks consistently so that they become habitual. In doing so, you will make procrastination far less likely.
- **Hypnosis:** This process rewires your brain's habit patterns, helping you create a more productive, efficient, and positive mindset and habit pattern that you can apply to your day-to-day life.

The truth about time management

Some people are under the misguided impression that time management means you have to do more in less time. The truth is that time management is not about cramming more tasks into your day. It is about doing the right tasks as efficiently as possible and prioritising what truly matters.

Focusing on quality over quantity is one of the key messages I find my clients need to hear in their hypnosis sessions. Always remember that achieving optimum time management is about achieving meaningful progress, not about being busy.

Another misconception I frequently encounter is that multitasking is an effective strategy for time management. However, multitasking often leads to reduced productivity and a lower quality of work, because bouncing between tasks splits your attention and can cause mental fatigue.

Instead, it is far better to practise what I term "single tasking", where you focus on one task at a time and avoid distractions that result in multitasking. Focusing on one thing at a time leads to better results and less stress.

Sometimes people tell me that they don't need to manage their time if they're not busy. But even if you are not overwhelmed with tasks, that doesn't mean you won't benefit from managing your time more effectively. In fact, doing so is key for making progress towards your long-term goals, and ensuring you have balance in your life.

When you plan your life during less busy periods, it will help you see opportunities to invest in personal development, give you a chance to reflect on your goals and perhaps tackle tasks that often get pushed aside during busier times. Remember, time management is about maximising your time, creating a more balanced and fulfilling life, not just handling business.

Time management also doesn't have to mean you need a strict schedule. While structure is important, if you go too far the other way and have an overly rigid schedule, you will face other challenges. These can include burnout and an inability to adapt to changes or unexpected events.

I always recommend allowing some flexibility in every day, by setting goals and prioritising them without being overly wedded to when in your day you complete those goals. It's important to allow some buffer time in your days so that you can absorb unexpected tasks and stay productive, without feeling constrained or stretched by an unnecessarily strict schedule.

I also encourage you to remember that time management is not only for work-related tasks. It applies to all areas of our lives, including personal time, hobbies, family and self-care, so it is best to integrate all aspects of your life into your time management plan. Make sure you prioritise time for relaxation, exercise and social activities, just as you would work tasks. This holistic combined approach prevents burnout, and ensures that you maintain a far better and healthier work-life balance.

There is no one-size-fits-all approach to time management. What works for one person might not work for another, so find what suits you best and tailor your approach to your own preferences. Be open to adjusting your strategy too, because what works for you can shift and change as your life does.

It's important to remember that even if you manage your time well, you can and will still feel stress. Even though effective time management can reduce stress, it won't eliminate it entirely. Life is unpredictable and as we all know, stress can arise from factors outside of your control. Recognising that stress is a normal part of life is healthy, and will allow you to see where you can use time management techniques to minimise avoidable stress.

Hypnotherapy, meditation and taking regular breaks can also further help you find the right balance and keep your stress levels as low as possible.

Although time management techniques can help you overcome procrastination, these techniques alone won't combat it effectively if you do not deal with the deeper psychological roots of your procrastination. You have to address a fear of failure, fear of success, perfectionism or a lack of motivation deep within your psyche, otherwise you will continue to procrastinate no matter what time management techniques you use.

This is why hypnotherapy is so valuable, because it helps you reprogram your subconscious and in doing so removes the root cause of your procrastination. This makes it easier for you to develop good habit patterns using the right time management techniques. Without addressing the root cause of the issue, however, time management strategies will only get you so far.

Dominic's story: avoiding the eleventh-hour trap

Dominic was a very bright IT professional who was just a few years into his career. He had a bright future ahead of him, but there was one challenge that threatened to derail his success – he would leave all of his projects until the very last minute.

Even if he had a project that should take several weeks, he would wait until the eleventh hour to get started. As a result, he'd have to work through the night and often would produce work that, although it was of a high enough standard, was not as good as it could have been had he spent a little longer working on it.

Of course, his method of operating at full power for short bursts of time also affected the balance in his life and caused stress. We used hypnosis to positively change the way he thought about his work projects and his deadlines. Over five sessions, we rewired his brain to help him recognise the value of starting projects earlier.

By the time we finished our sessions, Dominic was not only starting projects earlier, but often finishing them ahead of his deadlines. He told me that it was as though a weight had been lifted from his shoulders, and that he felt happier, calmer and more relaxed. He was also able to produce far better work.

The higher quality of his work was soon recognised at the company he worked for, where he received a better promotion than he had expected. One year on, when I touched base with him, I was delighted to hear that this new, positive habit pattern had stuck and that he was still thriving in his career with far less stress.

Why motivation is key to overcoming procrastination

Motivation provides the push we need to overcome any initial resistance to starting a task – such as the fears and emotions we discussed earlier in this chapter. Without motivation, we are highly unlikely to ever take the first step towards completing a task, and, therefore, we will become trapped in an unproductive cycle of procrastination.

But motivation isn't only crucial for initiating a task. It is also essential for sustaining progress, particularly in pursuit of long-term goals. Alongside motivation, you need to maintain focus and be persistent. Hypnosis can help with all of this. The hypnotic suggestion phase around motivation is especially useful in this regard, as it can help you to stay engaged with a task even when it's challenging or monotonous. This persistence is key to completing tasks, and avoiding negative habit patterns and temptation to procrastinate.

Motivation also helps us to build momentum because once we start a task and see progress, our motivation often increases, making it far easier to continue working. This positive feedback loop helps break the cycle of procrastination. You make headway on a project and as you see tangible results that sense of accomplishment can further fuel your motivation, reducing the likelihood of stopping or delaying work.

Being motivated also enhances your self-efficacy because motivation boosts your belief in your ability to succeed. When you're motivated, you're more likely to believe you can complete a task well, which in turn reduces procrastination driven by self-doubt.

Visualisation is a powerful tool to use to help motivate you and keep you on track. If you're motivated by a clear vision of success, like visualising yourself giving a successful presentation, you're more likely to believe in your ability to prepare thoroughly. This belief will prevent you putting off the preparation due to a fear of failing.

Combining action with goals is also key, as motivation connects your actions to your goals and values. When you understand how a task contributes to a larger goal, you're more likely to prioritise it and avoid procrastination. If my clients are motivated, for example, by the desire to advance in their career, which most of them are, they'll see completing a challenging work project is a step toward their goal, making it less likely that they'll delay the task.

Motivation also helps counteract negative emotions like anxiety and boredom, while instilling a sense of urgency, which is crucial for breaking the cycle of procrastination. When you feel driven to achieve something, you're more likely to act immediately rather than delaying.

Sustained motivation also prevents burnout by helping you manage your time and energy effectively. When you're motivated to succeed, you're more likely to plan your work and take breaks. This ensures you maintain a balance that keeps you productive without feeling overwhelmed or stressed. Staying motivated through regular rewards and recognition can keep your energy levels high and helps you maintain steady progress, preventing the risk of burnout that often leads to people falling back into the negative thought patterns that lead to procrastination.

I know how easy it can be to slip into procrastination, and in the early stages of building my hypnosis app, *Subconsciously*, I knew I'd need to use all my self-hypnosis tools and techniques to stay on track. I started building the app during the Covid-19 pandemic, when we were all coping with lockdowns and other disruption to our daily lives. Even though there were many technical problems initially, which required a lot of testing and bug fixing, I refused to put this work off.

It would have been easy for me to become frustrated and, therefore, to procrastinate and give up. While there were certainly periods of frustration, I made sure I maintained a positive focus on my end goal – to create one of the best hypnosis therapy apps available to benefit people all over the world in an affordable way. In doing so, I was able to tackle each challenge as it came up.

Instead of giving up, I employed the right people, asked the right questions and was able to stay motivated because of my positive focus on this bigger vision for the future.

Tips to stay motivated

As well as hypnosis, other practical steps you can take to immediately combat procrastination and stay motivated are:

- **Writing down your goals:** Writing goals down physically, using a pen and paper, psychologically imprints the goal in a more powerful and meaningful way. It's also essential to give yourself a deadline for achieving each of your goals, otherwise it is too easy to put them off indefinitely.
- **Break your goals down:** When you break a big goal into smaller chunks, it feels more manageable and becomes more

appealing. As a result, you are far less likely to procrastinate over getting started.
- **Visualise the future you want:** I'll share a visualisation exercise for you shortly, but the reason this works is because it helps you see what is possible if you stay motivated.

> **Time out: visualising future success**
>
> Take some time now. Close your eyes, and let's do an affirmation together. Take a deep breath, press together your thumb and middle finger. Repeat the following words to yourself, whilst imagining the emotions you will feel having ticked off and completed those things that you know need to be done.
>
> → I take action.
> → I succeed.
> → I am free from procrastination.
>
> Picture yourself in a favourite place, or a safe place, celebrating what you've accomplished with those you love and appreciate celebrating your success as well.
>
> Repeat those affirmations and visualise that scene a few times. When you're ready, open your eyes and start working towards your goal.

- **Harness your fear:** Fear is a powerful emotion and if we can harness it in a positive way, it can drive us to action. Take a moment to write down how you will feel six months from now if you do nothing towards your goal. Be brave and really honest with yourself about the cost of continuing your life without any action.
- **Build accountability:** On a practical level, you can enlist a support team to help you stay focused. This could be anyone you trust. The key to making this work is setting up a time to

check in regularly and being open about how your support team can help you stay focused.
- **Reward your progress:** Set up a reward system to ensure you celebrate progress, even small successes. Act bravely and know that taking consistent, regular action will help you build momentum.

The time to start is now. Don't put off what you can do today, remember that life rewards action.

> **Time out: affirmations for taking action**
>
> Take a moment now to pause, pressing your thumb and middle finger together and closing your eyes. Repeat the following to yourself:
>
> → I will take that first step now, today, life rewards action.
>
> Say that to yourself two or three times, then open your eyes and get ready to get started!

Recognise when your motivation is slipping, and act

If you feel you're starting to lose motivation for a particular task or objective in your life, whether at work or personally, it's important to take immediate steps to regain it before any kind of procrastination or cycle of avoidance sets in.

The following are some practical steps to quickly boost motivation.

- **Reconnect with your why:** Remind yourself why a task or goal is so important to you. Reflect on the bigger picture and the benefits of completing the task. Take a few

moments to write down the reasons you started this task in the first place.
- **Visualise the positive outcomes:** Use the exercise I shared with you earlier in the chapter to visualise your future success.
- **Break down the task:** If the task feels overwhelming, break it down into smaller, more manageable pieces. If you've already broken a task down and it still feels overwhelming, see if you can break it down further. You can create to-do lists with very specific tasks. Focus on completing one small part of the task, helping you to regain a sense of progress and momentum.
- **Set a micro-goal:** Setting small, immediate goals that you can achieve even in the next 10–15 minutes is a great way to regain momentum. Commit to working on the task for just ten minutes. Often starting is the hardest part, but once you begin it's easier to continue. After ten minutes, assess how you feel. Chances are, you'll feel motivated to keep going.
- **Change your environment:** Sometimes a change of scenery can boost motivation by breaking up the monotony and refreshing your perspective. You could move to a different room, go to a coffee shop or cafe, or just reorganise your workspace. A fresh environment can stimulate new energy, focus and drive, and mitigate the chances of procrastination kicking in.
- **Use positive self-talk:** Replace negative thoughts with positive affirmations to shift your mindset.
- **Reward yourself:** Set up small rewards for completing the next task or for working continuously for a set period. Promise yourself a break, a snack or a quick walk after completing a specific task. Knowing there's a reward at the end can make the work much more enticing.
- **Revisit past successes:** Remind yourself of times when you've overcome challenges or completed difficult tasks.

Reflect on those previous successes and how good it felt to accomplish those goals. This can help reignite your motivation and remind you that you're capable of finishing the current task.
- **Engage in a quick, energising activity:** Boosting your physical energy can help recharge your mental energy. Use the Pomodoro technique, working in short bursts with breaks in between to maintain that consistency of focus and prevent burnout and the risk of procrastination again setting in. Set a timer for 25 minutes, a Pomodoro, work on the task during that time and then take a five minute break. Repeat this cycle three to four times, then take a longer break. The structured time blocks can help you stay motivated and productive.
- **Talk it out:** Sometimes it is worth discussing the task or challenges with someone who can provide a new perspective and encouragement. This might mean calling a friend, colleague or a mentor to talk about what you're working on. Sometimes someone else showing interest in your progress is enough to give you a productivity boost.

Time out: affirmations for staying on track

Press together your thumb and middle finger as you let your eyes close and take two long, slow deep breaths. Repeat the following affirmations to yourself:

→ I use my time productively.
→ I am in the moment.
→ I make things happen.
→ I can do this.
→ Every small step counts.
→ I start and finish off tasks easily, confidently, in good time.

> Now visualise yourself at the end of the challenge or the task. It's completed. Bask in the sense of achievement, satisfaction and fulfilment you feel. Perhaps you can even see yourself getting the appreciation and recognition for completing that task from others, whether at work or in your personal life.
>
> Allow your eyes to open and enjoy knowing that you are taking control of your life, your time, your energy and your efficiency.

By using the techniques and advice I've shared in this chapter, procrastination can become a thing of the past. It will be something you used to do, but no longer. Remember, you don't need procrastination in your life, you don't want it, you won't have it, and you enjoy setting up this new habit pattern.

Part Three: Creating Lasting Change

In this final part of the book we're going to explore some additional tools and strategies you can use to create lasting change in your life. As you may have noticed, bringing balance to your life is one of the keys to feeling more fulfilled and happier. It is also essential for overcoming many of the challenges we've identified, such as breaking free of addiction, overcoming mental blockages and stopping procrastination.

So, creating greater balance in your life is where we begin in Chapter 7. We also look at the importance of adapting to change for our continued wellbeing. The world is changing faster than it ever has, which can be overwhelming. However, hypnotherapy techniques can help you to regain a sense of control and calm.

In the final chapter, I will share some more of my clients' stories to demonstrate just how much of a transformative impact hypnotherapy can have on your life. Many of my clients report feeling happier, healthier and more fulfilled after our sessions. I'd like you to feel that same sense of happiness, health and fulfilment in your own life.

Chapter Seven

Balancing Work, Aspirations and Family Life

Finding the balance between work, aspirations and family life is the central challenge for many of us in today's world. It's also one of the most common sources of anxiety and stress. As we live in such a fast-paced, technologically driven society, it's becoming increasingly hard to balance work and home life. Many of us struggle to find a healthy or ideal balance between our careers and our families. One is usually given greater priority.

Most of the time, careers and work seem to have that priority due to multiple factors such as fears of losing your job, not being appreciated enough, not progressing well enough or not working hard enough. Therefore, the family-work balance is one of the critical challenges to get right, if we want to achieve happier, healthier lives.

Finding balance is about more than just "fitting everything in". How well you manage to balance your competing priorities will ultimately affect what kind of life you'll live, how calm, rather than anxious, you'll feel, and how fulfilled you'll feel.

I'm not here to tell you what the "right" balance is, because this is very personal. The key is being true to yourself, identifying the balance you need to achieve, and identifying the patterns and habits that need to change to enable you to achieve that balance. This may take some time. You might have to adapt and test your approach to see which works best to deliver the balance you need from a combined mental, physical, financial, spiritual and family perspective. All I will say is that when you look back on your life, getting that balance right will likely be one of the main ways in which you judge the kind of life you've led.

Another reason why striking this balance is important is because not finding the right balance between work and family, or our personal lives can lead to other imbalances that either create mental health issues or exacerbate existing ones. Without balance, anxiety and stress increase. This has a domino effect that can lead to an increase in depression, low mood, absence from work and physical ill health.

However, too many of us attempt to fight through our imbalance. We tell ourselves that we can focus on our family, health or physical wellbeing "tomorrow". As a result we don't talk about or put great enough focus on our health, priorities and boundaries.

But there are real-world symptoms of imbalances in our lives that I see on a day-to-day basis, including drinking excessively, taking drugs, and exacerbating or even creating phobias. Some of these phobias relate to a person's health, which can then create fear about death, heart attack and other serious illnesses. This feeds into a vicious cycle that only gets worse over time. But all of this stems from not taking the need for work-life balance seriously.

Sonal's story: the strain of imbalance

When Sonal came into my consulting room, she told me that she felt she wasn't living. She had two children under the age of 21, and had frequent arguments with her husband, who was 15 years younger than her. When she looked at her life, she felt she hadn't had the opportunity to enjoy both a career and a social life.

As a result, resentment had built up, but she hid it from her family. Her coping mechanism became heavy drinking. In the last couple of years it had reached a point where it was a serious problem. Sonal would drink wine, whiskey or vodka every day, sometimes in secret.

Of course, the drinking only created a greater imbalance in her family life and although she had forged a successful career, her home life was poor. Life with her family was tense, and there were frequent, sometimes violent, arguments, all of which pointed to a deeply divided family.

Finding better balance was the key for Sonal to take control of her drinking issue and improve her relationship with both her husband and her children. This was what we worked on during our sessions together.

Be conscious of the need for balance

Achieving a work-life balance is often very challenging. The first step in the right direction is to make a conscious decision to achieve this balance. Without this conscious decision, you're much more likely to fail. But when you choose to place your focus on improving the balance in your life, you will find more opportunities to do so.

You also need to honestly assess your life to work out which parts you dedicate the most time and energy to, and which ones you neglect. As I've said, many people tend to focus on work at the expense of family. If you recognise that you've done the same, strengthening your bond with your family is an important place to start. Strong communication underpins your family relationships. Family relationships are a central strand for a happy and healthy work-life balance because it creates trust and demonstrates an understanding that this support network is important to you.

We need to be able to share about our lives with those who we are closest to. Sometimes this may mean communicating about any stress, anxiety or pressure we're facing in the workplace, as well as any positive achievements.

Another good way to start introducing a better balance between your work and home life is to work more flexibly. Since the Covid-19 pandemic, working from home has become much more common. Having this option can make it much easier to balance your professional and personal responsibilities.

However, it's essential to recognise that you won't be able to create this sense of balance on your own, so let those around you help you. Friends, family and other trusted individuals can take some of the load off of you by handling tasks like taking your children to school or sports practices, for example, or even walking your dog once in a while.

Time out: focus on your health

When you are working to achieve a better balance, it's essential that you prioritise your own health. Ultimately, if you don't have a healthy mind and body, you won't be able to properly focus on either your work or your personal life.

So, take a pen and paper and write:

→ Health comes above all.

Now close your eyes, press your thumb and middle finger together and take two deep, long breaths. Then repeat the following affirmations to yourself two to three times:

→ I prioritise my health, my time and my life.
→ I focus on a healthy diet, daily exercise and better sleep.

Open your eyes and think about how you can improve your diet, do some exercise or ensure you get better quality sleep today.

I can share one top tip with you now – take a break from technology. If you have your phone near you while you're reading this book, put it on the other side of the room instead, or even in another room entirely. It's good to set aside specific intervals during the day, during which you distance yourself from your phone and instead dedicate time to yourself and your family.

There are many studies that show taking a break from technology improves your awareness, sleep patterns, emotional regulation and human connections. A great way to do this with your whole family is to have game nights, where you play board games that don't require technology. Turn your phones off or put them in another room and enjoy focusing on the game and spending time with one another.

Communication: a foundational skill

Communication skills are crucial in every aspect of life, both personally and professionally. Communication ensures that ideas, information and basic instructions are conveyed clearly and accurately, so there are no misunderstandings.

Strong communication promotes teamwork, good spirit, collaboration and efficiency in workplaces, classrooms and our daily interactions. Clear communication is also essential for the health of our relationships, professional or personal, because it helps to establish trust and understanding. Strong relationships are built through open dialogue and the ability to express thoughts and emotions effectively.

In professional environments, communication skills are the key to effective teamwork, negotiation, leadership and conflict resolution. They help individuals present ideas convincingly and allow us to navigate challenges essential for career growth. I help a lot of clients who, due to confidence and anxiety issues, feel they can't communicate their true desires or thoughts. Being unable to communicate their true desires and thoughts impedes their progress, stunts their career growth and means they enjoy their time at work less than they otherwise would.

Within teams, effective communication helps us to identify problems and find solutions by encouraging everyone involved to share their perspectives. Collaborative discussions also aid our decision-making processes and ensure that all relevant information is considered before a decision is made.

Clear and empathetic communication helps us to resolve all manner of disagreements by addressing concerns directly. People who communicate their thoughts, needs and emotions effectively also tend to have much better mental health, because expressing yourself reduces stress and promotes emotional wellbeing.

Communication is also essential for influencing others and persuading them to see a different perspective or take a particular course of action. This is particularly valuable for many of my clients, who are leaders, founders or directors at the top of their game. They know clear communication is valuable for their leadership, negotiation and for marketing their businesses.

I often help business leaders to communicate challenging news, such as letting people go or making redundancies. During our sessions around such topics, I help the leader in question boost their confidence around communicating this kind of decision, as well as helping them create a balance between empathy, fairness and directness in the way they deliver such news. This helps them avoid experiencing excessive emotions themselves, while acknowledging the emotions others may be feeling.

A study published in the *International Journal of Management Studies* found that leaders with strong communication skills are more effective at motivating teams, increasing the satisfaction amongst their staff and improving overall organisational performance.[16] Communication competence was identified as one of the key attributes to successful leadership.

In an increasingly globalised world, effective communication also helps bridge cultural differences. Understanding and adapting to different communication styles is vital in diverse work environments and multicultural societies. Effective communication within teams also helps members of the team stay aligned with key goals, objectives and responsibilities, and fosters genuine collaboration. This leads to smoother workflows and ensures that everyone is singing from the same hymn sheet, as the saying goes.

---

16 Dr Lal S., *View of communication: an effective leadership skill* (Jan 2019). International Journal of Management Studies, https://researchersworld.com/index.php/ijms/article/view/2239/2097.

There have been many studies published around the benefits of good communication. In a 2011 study, top consulting firm McKinsey & Company found that effective communication within teams significantly improved (by over 50 per cent) group performance and cohesion. The research showed that teams with clear, open lines of communication were more likely to achieve their goals and navigate conflicts effectively.[17]

On a personal level, being able to articulate your thoughts clearly boosts your self-esteem and confidence, allowing you to project competence and self-assuredness. This applies whether you are speaking publicly, or having interpersonal conversations.

What's also interesting is that nonverbal communication is just as, if not more, important than verbal communication, particularly during the learning process. A study in the *Journal of Educational Psychology* highlighted the importance of nonverbal communication, noting that teachers who use gestures and eye contact effectively can make their students more engaged and enhance their understanding of what's being taught.[18]

It is clear that being able to openly communicate with others can also have a positive impact on our mental health. As you can see, there is a great deal of scientific research that overwhelmingly supports the critical role communication plays in improving our performance, relationships and wellbeing within a range of settings.

---

[17] humansmart.com.mx (2024) *What impact does effective communication have on team performance in the workplace?* https://humansmart.com.mx/en/blogs/blog-what-impact-does-effective-communication-have-on-team-performance-in-the-workplace-56539.

[18] Abekah Keelson, S., Odei Addo, J. and Dodor, A. (2024) 'The influence of lecturer non-verbal cues on student perceptions of teaching quality: the role of gender and age', *Cogent Education*, 11(1). doi: 10.1080/2331186X.2024.2325788.

Part Three: Creating Lasting Change

Communication and conflict resolution

Effective communication is essential for reducing conflicts both in family and work settings. When you communicate well and you convey your message clearly, you minimise the misunderstandings that so often lead to conflict and unnecessary arguments. One study found that couples who communicate effectively are far more successful in resolving conflicts and report far higher relationship satisfaction.[19]

Clear communication in any kind of relationship helps both parties understand each other's perspectives, needs and expectations, and bolsters a sense of common empathy and understanding. Open and honest communication also fosters trust among family members and colleagues. This forms the foundation of any strong and healthy relationship, which in turn makes it much easier to resolve conflicts when they arise.

Among the most important communication skills for resolving and preventing conflict are active listening and empathising with others. In addition, when you are able to manage your own emotions effectively, you respond better to others' emotions and in doing so prevent conflicts from escalating.

Of course, conflict is a natural part of life, so the key is to ensure that when conflicts arise, we handle them in such a way that we achieve the best possible outcome for all involved. Effective communication is essential for conflict management because it facilitates a collaborative problem-solving approach. Individuals who can communicate well are more likely to engage in constructive

---

19   Ünal, Özge & Akgün, Serap. (2022). Relationship of Conflict Resolution Styles in Marriage with Marital Adjustment and Satisfaction. Psikiyatride Guncel Yaklasimlar - Current Approaches in Psychiatry.

Subconsciously

dialogue that focuses on solutions, rather than assigning blame and creating a blame-mindset atmosphere.

Improved communication also helps to reduce assumptions and speculations about others' intentions or actions. By asking clarifying questions and engaging in open dialogue, people can gain a much better understanding of the situation in front of them. Asking questions is only one step though, because you also need to actively listen to the answers to ensure you are taking all the information onboard.

Within individual relationships, consistent and effective communication leads to stronger bonds, which can make conflict resolution much more straightforward, and make it more likely that those involved will work towards a mutually beneficial solution.

Open communication also helps you to identify potential issues early on, allowing proactive measures to be taken before full-blown arguments emerge. Respect and inclusivity are other key factors, as effective communicators are usually good at respecting diverse viewpoints and encouraging inclusive discussions. This can reduce tensions that arise from people feeling unheard or misunderstood.

When you don't feel heard or as though you are misunderstood, anger is one of the most common emotions to arise. I frequently help clients with anger management issues. These individuals often find that the red mist descends before they have fully processed what's happening. In our work together, I help them take a step back from the situation and get them to pause, if only for a second, to recognise that instead of responding with anger, they need to communicate how they are feeling in a calm and respectful way.

Anger often blocks effective communication on both sides of the dialogue. When we feel angry we tend to find it harder to communicate our thoughts clearly, while those on the receiving end of anger will often become defensive and may stop listening to what's being said. This means that what might be a fair, valid or valuable point is either not communicated properly, or ignored because it is inextricably linked with anger.

Advice for improving communication

The following are some of the best ways in which you can improve your communication, whether with members of your family, friends or colleagues:

- **Active listening:** This is a vital skill, where you focus fully on the speaker, avoid interrupting, and ask clarifying questions to show that you understand. This builds trust and helps avoid misunderstandings. You can also summarise key points back to the person who was speaking to ensure your understanding.
- **Use nonverbal cues:** These can include nodding or making eye contact to demonstrate engagement.
- **Avoid over complicating your message:** This is true whether in conversation or writing. It's best to be direct and to the point, sticking to the essential points you want to cover, especially in work settings.
- **Use "I" statements:** "I" statements are particularly useful when discussing difficult topics, as you can use them to express your feelings without sounding accusatory. For example, instead of saying, "You never listen…" you could say, "I feel unheard when we talk and it frustrates me."
- **Encourage feedback:** Be willing to adjust your communication style if needed. After sharing your thoughts, ask, "Does this make sense to you?" In doing so you ensure clarity. You could also ask, "How do you feel about this?" to invite responses and show openness.

- **In intense situations try to remain calm and patient:** Reacting emotionally can escalate conflicts whereas staying composed leads to far better resolution. Take a deep breath, pause before responding and avoid offensive body language or harsh tones.
- **Pay attention to your body language, facial expressions and tone of voice:** These nonverbal cues can either support or undermine what you are saying. Make eye contact, avoid crossing your arms and use a friendly tone to convey warmth and openness.
- **Show empathy by considering the other person's feelings and perspectives:** Use phrases like, "I understand this is important to you", or "It sounds like you're feeling frustrated, let's talk about how we can fix this."
- **Set clear boundaries:** In both family and work contexts clear boundaries can prevent misunderstandings and foster much healthier communication. Set expectations for how and when communication should happen, such as by saying, "Let's discuss this in our meeting", or "We'll talk more about this at dinner."
- **Choose your moment:** Choosing the right moment for important conversations is essential. Timing can affect how well your message is received, so avoid starting serious discussions when someone is stressed or distracted. Before you begin, ask if it's a good time to talk about something important.
- **Use technology to enhance communication:** Emails, messaging apps and video calls can be really useful tools when used appropriately.
- **Don't wait for a problem to give feedback:** Regularly offering positive feedback often strengthens bonds and motivates improvement. Recognise other people's efforts by saying things like, "I appreciate how you handled that", or "Great job on this task."

Time out: affirmations to become a better communicator

Let your eyes close, take a nice deep breath and press together your thumb and middle finger. Then repeat the following affirmations to yourself two to three times:

→ I communicate confidently, clearly and consistently.
→ I am comfortable and confident communicating to anyone, anytime, anywhere.

Once you have repeated those affirmations a few times, open your eyes and continue with your day. These can be useful ahead of any difficult conversations you need to have.

Samira's story: replacing anxiety with confident communication

When Samira came to see me, she was experiencing a great deal of anxiety about communicating in the workplace. She was returning to the corporate world after her maternity leave and in the time she had been off, had developed a fear around communicating with her peers.

The problem was, her anxiety was also impacting her ability to listen. This created even more anxiety – so she became trapped in a cycle of anxiety whereby she wasn't able to listen fully, but that in turn made her more anxious because she hadn't heard or absorbed what was said. This would feed her anxiety when speaking, because she knew she wasn't fully engaged in the conversation.

All of this anxiety compounded to the point that her ability to communicate her thoughts and ideas to the other members of her team was being severely impacted. We did four sessions of hypnosis to help her achieve a positive state in which she could control her anxiety and in doing so feel calm about listening. This then gave her the confidence to contribute to discussions.

By focusing on her communication skills, we were able to build her confidence and dramatically improve her life from a personal perspective, as well as benefiting her career.

The importance of boundaries

Establishing boundaries between work and family life is important. Boundaries hold the line between determining which actions we deem to be acceptable and which are unacceptable. It's valuable to know what your non-negotiable boundaries are, or if you don't currently have any, to set some.

Over the years, many clients have come to me with issues around boundaries, and more specifically not being able to properly set boundaries in their lives. If this sounds familiar, then take your time with this section. Setting boundaries is essential for maintaining personal time and balancing responsibilities because boundaries help you prioritise your needs, manage stress and maintain healthier relationships.

Without clear boundaries you may feel pressured to take on too many responsibilities, whether at work or personally. This often leads to physical and mental exhaustion or burnout. By setting limits on how much time and energy you devote to work, social obligations and family, you can ensure you have time for rest and self-care, which helps prevent burnout.

Constantly being available or over-committed also causes stress and anxiety, but without clear boundaries you may feel like you're always on call. This negatively impacts your emotional wellbeing. Setting clear expectations about when you're available or how much you can take on allows you to protect your mental and emotional health, giving you that space to recharge your batteries.

When you understand that boundaries are essential for protecting your mental health, it becomes easier to set them. This is why this messaging is a key component of the hypnotic suggestions I use with my clients, because it gives them the confidence to set and keep boundaries consistently. In the process this helps them lead a much happier, freer, calmer and healthier life.

The dangers of not setting boundaries

When you don't set boundaries others may unintentionally take advantage of your time or energy. Typically this leads to feelings of resentment or frustration on your part which further harm personal or professional relationships.

By being upfront about your limits, you teach others how to interact with you respectfully. This creates far more balanced relationships where your needs and the needs of others are equally respected. If you constantly say yes to others' requests at the expense of your own needs, you may start to feel overwhelmed. Many of my clients feel like they've been taken for granted. Over time this impacts their self-worth and reduces their self-esteem. Setting and enforcing boundaries, however, shows that you respect yourself.

All too often, we believe our needs should come second to the needs of others, but this perspective indicates a lack of self-respect. Again, this is a common challenge I help my clients address through our work together. By building up their self-confidence and self-respect, I make it easier for them to set and maintain the boundaries that are necessary for living a balanced and fulfilled life.

Without boundaries, it's easy to over-commit to various tasks, leaving you with little time for personal priorities or relaxation. If a lack of boundaries also mixes with poor time management, you're likely to miss deadlines and increase your stress levels.

If you're constantly juggling responsibilities without clear boundaries, your attention may also be scattered, reducing your productivity in all areas of life. Without boundaries you are more likely to feel obligated to say yes to everything, even when it negatively impacts your wellbeing. This often leads to feelings of guilt because you can't do it all. What's more, when you don't set boundaries, your personal time is usually the first thing you sacrifice. Again this speaks to putting others' needs before your own. The outcome is little time for self-care, hobbies and personal development.

In today's fast-paced world it's easy for work to spill into personal life, especially with the rise of remote work. Without boundaries you may find yourself working late into the night or during weekends. Therefore, setting boundaries is vital for protecting your time, energy and wellbeing, as well as for prioritising personal care, and maintaining healthier and more balanced relationships.

But there is evidence that a lack of boundaries, particularly between our work and personal lives, has a negative effect on our physical and mental wellbeing. A study by the CIPD (Chartered Institute of Personnel and Development) in 2019 found that poor work-life balance is associated with far higher levels of stress, anxiety and depression than other mental health issues.[20]

---

20   The CIPD et al. (2019) *Health and well-being at work*. https://www.councilforworkandhealth.org.uk/wp-content/uploads/2019/05/CIPD-health-and-well-being-at-work-2019_tcm18-55881.pdf.

Meanwhile, a 2018 study in *Current Cardiology Report* revealed that people who work long hours without sufficient personal time are at far higher risk of developing cardiovascular diseases.[21] Overworking yourself is also linked to higher rates of obesity, diabetes and other physical health conditions.

On the other side of the coin, research published in the *Journal of Vocational Behaviour*, showed employees who are able to maintain boundaries between work and personal life tend to be far more satisfied with their jobs and quality of life, reducing anxiety and depression rates. The researchers used a sample of 1,416 employees from seven distinct populations – Malaysian, Chinese, New Zealand Maori, New Zealand European, Spanish, French, and Italian. It also highlighted that this work-life balance benefit was even more pronounced in cultures of greater gender equality and more individualistic cultures.[22]

Finally, a study in 2017 titled "Family Relationships and Wellbeing" and published in *Innovation in Ageing*, revealed that individuals who dedicate sufficient time to their personal lives and balance family relationships, report far stronger emotional bonds with their children.[23] These individuals are also more likely to experience positive family dynamics and lower levels of conflict.

---

21 Virtanen, M. and Kivimäki, M. (2018) 'Long working hours and risk of cardiovascular disease,' *Current Cardiology Reports*, 20(11). https://doi.org/10.1007/s11886-018-1049-9.

22 Jarrod M. Haar, Marcello Russo, Albert Suñe, Ariane Ollier-Malaterre, (2014) 'Outcomes of work–life balance on job satisfaction, life satisfaction and mental health: A study across seven cultures,' *Journal of Vocational Behavior*, Volume 85, Issue 3, Pages 361-373, ISSN 0001-8791, https://doi.org/10.1016/j.jvb.2014.08.010

23 Thomas, P.A., Liu, H. and Umberson, D. (2017) 'Family Relationships and Well-Being,' *Innovation in Aging*, 1(3). https://doi.org/10.1093/geroni/igx025

Amir's story: from burnout to balance

Amir was a top-level director in the banking industry in London, who was not managing his workload or balancing his personal and professional lives well. Amir would often wake up during the night, as he was dealing with prices and stocks right across the world in various time zones, from the US to the Asian markets. This was creating a cycle of panic attacks. Fear of the panic itself was only making it worse.

Amir burnt out, which meant that even when he took personal time, he was fatigued both mentally and physically. The cycle of panic and fear was also impacting him psychosexually. In short, it was affecting every part of his life.

When he came to see me, he was struggling with his burnout, feeling the pressure of being at the top of his industry, while also going through a bitter divorce. We had five sessions of hypnosis together during which time I rewired and reprogrammed his brain to help him develop a calmness, balance and the ability to separate his work and personal lives. This helped him not to take what happened at work too seriously, and allowed him to start enjoying his life again.

By the end of our second session, Amir looked as though a 100-ton weight had lifted from his shoulders. His transformation from a burnt out and broken man into one who could see the light, happened incredibly quickly. He felt a new sense of optimism and was able to appreciate his efforts and talent at work.

He went from low to high; unbalanced to balanced; panic-stricken to in control of his anxiety. It was a complete transformation.

Setting boundaries isn't selfish

Too many people feel guilty when they establish limits on their time, energy or emotional capacity. They believe they are neglecting others or not meeting expectations, but setting boundaries allows you to give more to others and exceed expectations. After all, if you're not taking care of your own wellbeing you will have less to give to others. So, if you feel that setting boundaries makes you selfish, I'd like you to change your perspective right now.

Setting boundaries is essential for maintaining healthy relationships and being able to support others. You can't effectively help others if you are burnt out, overwhelmed or emotionally drained yourself. When you set clear boundaries, you prevent misunderstandings. You reduce resentment and create far more meaningful and balanced relationships. This benefits both you and the people around you because it leads to far clearer communication and mutual respect.

Establishing limits on how much you give does not mean you are isolating yourself or cutting others off. Rather, it ensures you have enough energy for personal growth, self-care and the ability to be present and engaged when interacting with others.

Advice for establishing boundaries

If you struggle to establish boundaries, then you are certainly not alone. What's more, establishing and maintaining boundaries can be challenging if you are not used to it. The following are some practical tips to help you establish boundaries and stick to them. At the end of this chapter, I'll also share some affirmations you can use to help reprogram and rewire your brain.

- **Start with small, manageable boundaries:** Set small boundaries in less stressful situations to begin with if you find setting boundaries overwhelming. This will help build your confidence over time.
- **Create time blocks around your communication:** If you're the kind of person who is always available to answer messages or emails, start by waiting 30 minutes to respond to any message you receive. Gradually work your way up to creating specific time blocks for communication from different sources. For example, build up so that you no longer respond to emails outside of working hours.
- **Reflect:** Take time to reflect on what areas of your life feel overwhelming, or where you most frequently feel drained or burnt out. This will help you identify where boundaries are most needed. Ask yourself questions like when do I feel most anxious or taken advantage of or taken for granted? Where do I feel like I need more personal space or time?
- **Be direct, but respectful:** This is crucial when setting boundaries. Remember you don't have to explain every detail. All that is required is that you make your needs clear. For example, if someone asks you for help at work, instead of jumping in, say, "I can help you with this task for 30 minutes, but then I need to focus on my work."
- **Practice saying "No":** Many of my clients find it very hard to say "no" whether in personal relationships or in their professional ones. Saying "no" can be very difficult, especially if you're used to people pleasing, but it's essential to say no if you want to set boundaries. Start by saying "no" in low stakes situations to build your comfort level. For instance, if someone asks you for a favour when you're struggling with time, you can simply say, "I'm not

able to help that right now." Avoid over-explaining or apologising. When discussing your boundaries, use "I" statements, as I explained earlier, to keep the focus on your feelings rather than blaming or criticising the other person.
- **Be consistent:** Consistency is key to maintaining boundaries. If you set a boundary, but then regularly bend or break it people will stop respecting it.

It's normal to feel uncomfortable when setting boundaries, especially at first. Remind yourself that boundaries are necessary for your wellbeing. Stick by the boundaries you set and you'll find your discomfort will lessen over time. You'll also start to experience the benefits of having boundaries and a better balance in your life, which will make it easier to set boundaries in the future.

Be prepared that some people may resist your boundaries, especially if they're used to you always saying "yes" or being available. Stay firm without feeling guilty. If someone pushes back when you set a boundary, repeat your stance calmly. Use phrases like, "I understand this is important, but I really need to focus on my work now. Let's find another time when I can help you." The more you do this, the more confident you will become with setting boundaries and the easier it will be to establish and stick to them.

Sometimes it helps to talk to a trusted friend, mentor or therapist if you are struggling with setting boundaries. Naturally I would recommend hypnotherapy, as this is very quick-acting and long-lasting therapy. However you choose to seek support, acknowledge and celebrate your small victories along the way. Setting boundaries is a process and it's important to recognise the progress you're making.

Time out: building confidence with boundary setting

Close your eyes now and let's do a little bit of affirmation. Take a nice couple of deep breaths. Inhale relaxation into mind and body. Exhale any tension. Press together your thumb and middle finger. Now repeat the following affirmations two to three times:

→ I respect my own personal time and space.
→ I enforce my boundaries confidently, clearly and consistently.
→ I feel no guilt.
→ I feel positive setting and keeping to my boundaries.

Open your eyes and return to these affirmations as often as you need.

Chapter Eight

Adapting to Modern Challenges and Embracing Change

The modern world throws many new challenges at us that we need to navigate. Since the turn of the 21st century, we have seen technology change the world in which we live in ways that would have been unimaginable even 50 years ago. From the internet and smartphones to social media, the world in which we live has simultaneously become more connected and more distracting.

Of course, in 2020 the Covid-19 pandemic hit the world and this has created a lasting impact on many of us. Prolonged periods of physical isolation and lockdowns left their mark on each of us in different ways. Never has it been so important for us, as individuals, to be able to adapt to and embrace change.

Managing screen time and digital distractions

For all that modern technology gives us, it also brings its own challenges and problems. For example, we know that excessive screen time is linked to increased anxiety, depression and stress. We also know that for some people, it can even lead to self-harm or suicide. This isn't just about the amount of time we spend looking at screens, but about the sites we visit and content we consume when we're on our digital devices.

Managing screen time is, therefore, essential for our mental health. We need to balance our time in the digital world with activities in the physical world to promote relaxation, and a healthy focus on our minds. Activities like reading (a physical book), exercising and spending time outdoors in nature can all help us reset mentally.

Similarly, spending too much time on screens can negatively impact our physical health if we aren't balancing time spent sedentary with exercise. Too much time on digital screens can result in issues including poor posture, eye strain and even disturbed sleep. When we manage our screen time effectively, we reduce the risk of developing such issues and promote a healthier lifestyle.

Digital distractions can also significantly hinder productivity. They promote increased levels of procrastination, making it difficult to focus on tasks and complete them efficiently. By setting clear boundaries around screen time throughout the day and sticking to them, we can improve our concentration and effectiveness both in work and personal projects, in a remarkable way.

When it comes to social connections, whilst digital devices play an important part in connecting us with others, excessive use can also lead to social isolation. Therefore, part of managing our screen time should include taking breaks from our devices for face-to-face interactions. In making sure we spend time together in person, we can foster deeper and more meaningful relationships.

It's particularly important to manage screen time for any children or adolescents in your life. Excessive use can impact cognitive development, attention span and, of course, academic performance. While it is important for all children and young people, monitoring and closely managing time spent on digital devices is especially crucial for those diagnosed with ADHD or ADD. By setting boundaries around digital devices for the young people in your life, you are encouraging them to develop a balanced approach to life in an increasingly digital world, which nurtures healthy development and learning.

Understanding when and how to use technology effectively is part of digital literacy, so it shouldn't be avoided completely. However, the key is to consciously manage screen time to help young people develop much better habits and make more intentional choices about their digital consumption.

Of course, many of us could do with a better balance between our time spent on and off digital devices as adults too. Achieving a healthy balance between screen time and other activities is absolutely essential for our overall wellbeing.

Finding that balance allows us to pursue hobbies, spend time with loved ones and engage in activities that fulfil us far beyond anything the digital realm could or can do. I have no doubt that, in the future, striking the right balance will become even more of a challenge as digital tech becomes even more realistic and pervasive in our lives.

Tips for effectively managing your screen time

It's essential for all of us to find effective ways to manage our screen time so that our mental and emotional wellbeing doesn't suffer. The following are some tips to help you gain better control over your digital device usage that will ultimately help you create healthier minds and bodies, and lead healthier, happier lives.

- **Track your usage:** Before you make any changes, it's important to understand your own habits around digital devices and screen time. Use the apps already available on most devices to help you track your screen time so that you can understand, and then adjust, your habits.
- **Set time limits:** Set specific time limits for using different devices or applications. You can use settings on your phone or computer to track your usage and set limits on certain apps.
- **Have screen-free times of day:** Designate certain times as screen-free zones. During meals and an hour before bedtime is advisable. Having times set aside for screen-free pursuits can also encourage more mindful and restful activities. You might find listening to some of the recordings on my app, *Subconsciously*, helps you.
- **Establish screen-free areas:** At home, it is a good idea to have screen-free zones, such as the dining room or bedrooms. That way you can set clear boundaries for everyone in your household and ensure that everyone is getting a break from their digital devices. Use these spaces to encourage other forms of interaction and relaxation.
- **Identify tasks that require a screen:** There is no escaping the fact that we need to use digital devices in our daily lives. Identify the essential tasks that require a screen and allocate time for them. Limit the use of your devices for leisure until those tasks are complete.
- **Turn off non-essential notifications:** This will minimise distractions and interruptions while you are using your device for specific, important tasks.
- **Schedule physical activity into your week:** Allocate times in your schedule for physical activity to break up your screen use. This can help reduce eye strain and improve your overall wellbeing.
- **Practise the 20-20-20 rule:** To reduce eye strain, take a 20 second break every 20 minutes to look at something

20 feet away. This gives your eyes a much-needed rest. The adjustment between looking at a screen and looking at something further away helps relax the eye muscles, reducing fatigue and eye strain. Trust me, that really does work well.
- **Avoid using multiple screens at once:** For example, don't watch TV while browsing on your phone. Instead, focus on one task at a time to enhance your concentration and experience.
- **Have screen-free days:** If you can, take a day off of all digital devices every now and then. Use this time to engage in activities that don't involve technology, such as reading, hiking, spending time with family and friends, or meditating. You could listen to some audio of hypnosis exercises, but avoid looking at a screen. Going screen-free might sound like a big ask, but reports indicate that it produces good results for mind, body, happiness, focus, sleep and relaxation.

I mentioned the 20-20-20 rule in that list of tips, and this is a great one to start with. One study published in the *Journal of Education and Health Promotion* documented that staring at screens for prolonged periods can lead to symptoms like headaches, dry eyes and blurred vision, (collectively known as computer vision syndrome or digital eye strain).[24]

Other research also supports these findings, showing that taking regular breaks from screen activities helps alleviate symptoms of eye strain. Firth et al. conducted a study, which showed that digital detox programs can improve mental health outcomes, such as reduced stress and anxiety, and often also lead to improved

---

24 Devi, K.A. and Singh, S.K. (2023) 'The hazards of excessive screen time: Impacts on physical health, mental health, and overall well-being,' *Journal of Education and Health Promotion*, 12(1). https://doi.org/10.4103/jehp.jehp_447_23.

physical health outcomes, such as weight loss and improved sleep.[25]

The impact of the Covid-19 pandemic on global mental health

The Covid-19 pandemic has significantly and continues to significantly impact mental health worldwide with a multitude of factors contributing to increased psychological distress across various societies and populations.

The uncertainty and fear of illness, and disruptions, caused by the pandemic have led to a rise in anxiety and depression levels globally. Many people have experienced heightened worries about health and finances in the future. Lockdowns and social distancing measures, along with remote working and schooling led to increased social isolation and loneliness. This lack of social interaction and support also negatively impacted mental health for many individuals.

There were, of course, some people who found the lockdowns and societal changes brought about by the Covid-19 pandemic preferable to "normal" life. However, for the vast majority of us, the overall impact was negative. A lack of human interaction caused issues mentally, emotionally and physically for many people.

The pandemic also caused significant economic disruption, leading in some cases to job losses and financial instability. Although some countries, such as the UK, had a government-led furlough scheme,

---

[25] Firth J, Torous J, Yung AR. Digital detoxification: A systematic review and meta-analysis of randomized controlled trials Psychiatry Res 20192731–930634110

there were many people in the world for whom the pandemic caused considerable financial instability and uncertainty. Increased stress about economic security has only contributed to further mental health challenges for many people.

Of course, many families faced the loss of loved ones due to Covid-19, and the grieving process was disrupted by their inability to hold normal funerals or gather in person. Again, this had a deep impact on people's emotional wellbeing.

There were also some groups within society, such as healthcare workers, frontline staff and individuals with pre-existing physical and/or mental health conditions who faced unique stresses and heightened mental health challenges due to a massively increased workload, exposure risk, and limited access to help and resources.

The pandemic also disrupted mental health services and reduced access to care for many individuals who really needed extra help, making it more difficult for people to seek support or ongoing treatment. Shifts to remote working also blurred the boundaries between professional and personal life, leading to increased workloads, burnout and stress. This was often exacerbated by the challenges of managing home responsibilities simultaneously.

School closures and remote learning also significantly impacted children and adolescents, leading to increased anxiety and difficulties with learning, as well as concerns about social development. These experiences had a particularly profound effect on more vulnerable children and adolescents.

In some cases, the stress and isolation of the pandemic led to increased use of alcohol and other substances as a coping mechanism. I recall a number of my clients who never used to drink, suddenly starting to drink regularly during the pandemic due to a combination of boredom and feeling like a prisoner in their own homes. Some of them would crack open a bottle of wine or a beer as early as lunchtime, even though they would never have dreamed of doing so prior to the lockdown.

Then there were the people who were already doing cocaine and other illicit drugs. Many of my clients with drug issues reported that during the pandemic, their cocaine use massively increased. This led to further mental and physical health issues, as well as deepening addiction and dependency issues.

Of course, for all of the challenges the pandemic brought and issues it caused people, both in terms of their physical, mental and emotional wellbeing, there were many people who managed to navigate pandemic-related stress successfully, without turning to drink or drugs to help them through those unprecedented times.

Lily's story: overcoming physical health challenges against the odds

By the time Lily came to see me, she had been suffering from a severe physical reaction to receiving the Covid-19 vaccine for three months. She was a doctor who, although she had reservations about having the vaccine due to her reactions to other vaccinations in the past, decided to take the Covid-19 vaccine, as many in her profession did.

However, within minutes it negatively affected her. The side effects only worsened over the days and weeks that followed. Her body overreacted to a multitude of things that previously would have caused her no issues. She experienced severe itchy, raw rashes breaking out all over her body, causing unbearable itching, excruciating irritations and blistering on the skin on much of her body. This could be set off by any kind of product, or even water at the wrong temperature.

When she came to see me, she had been off work for three months as a result of the ongoing issues she was having with her physical health. Mentally, she was in a bad way. In addition to having to deal with her own challenges, she was also responsible for caring for her parents, who were elderly and unwell themselves. However, she had faith that the hypnosis would work for her, and she was very open-minded to the process.

During our sessions we focused on helping her remain resolute, balanced and as calm as possible. The aim was to minimise her mental reactions to the irritations she faced. So often, our mind can make physical phenomena worse, so we worked on calming her mind in order to calm her physical body.

Through the hypnosis, we reprogrammed and rewired the connections between her mind and body and, sure enough, as she became calmer and processed the stress she had been under, her physical symptoms dissipated.

Lily also told me that she had been considering moving to Florida, where her brother lived, and starting over. For many years, she had procrastinated over making the move, but our hypnosis sessions helped her remove this block too. She realised she needed to put her parents into a care home, where they could receive the care they needed, and she let go of her guilt about doing so.

By helping her put her mind in a more positive, calm state, she experienced fewer physical and physiological overreactions and was able to rebuild her life. Lily's story is an excellent example of how our minds and bodies are inextricably interlinked.

Strategies for dealing with post-pandemic anxiety

One of the best pieces of advice I can give you for dealing with post-pandemic anxiety is to limit your exposure to news and social media. This is a positive habit to get into for many reasons, as constant exposure to negative news tends to increase anxiety and can lead to feelings of overwhelm around worst-case scenarios.

Anxiety often stems from a feeling of helplessness or being overwhelmed by uncertainties. Therefore, focusing on what you can control, not what you can't, helps you reclaim a sense of autonomy, power and agency. From a practical point of view, you could make a list of things you can influence, perhaps in a daily journal. This will help bring your focus into a more positive space.

Uncertainty can also disrupt our daily routines, leading to feelings of instability. Creating structure helps restore that sense of normalcy and predictability. Using daily routines that include the likes of work, self-care, relaxation and hobbies, as well as sticking to regular sleep patterns, eating healthy meals and exercise schedules provides stability and helps to reduce anxiety levels.

Listening to hypnotherapy, meditation and mindfulness recordings on a regular basis, such as those on my *Subconsciously* app, is a great way to reinforce and create new and positive changes in your life.

Whatever you choose to do to help address your pandemic-related anxiety, know that taking action is beneficial. If we leave our stress and anxiety to go unchecked, it will build to unmanageable levels and could even trigger post-traumatic stress disorder (PTSD).

If you lost loved ones and were unable to go through traditional mourning practices as a result of the restrictions in force at the height of the pandemic, you may be experiencing prolonged traumatic grief. You could, therefore, benefit from seeking some support to overcome this and put you in a more positive mental space.

I know how traumatic some of the experiences we all had during the pandemic could be. My now ex-partner became seriously ill with Covid-19, due to a weakened immune system. At one point, she could not speak properly and became a little delusional due to the lack of oxygen in her body. She was told by one doctor that if her breathlessness continued to the next day, she'd need to be hospitalised and put on a ventilator.

This was a scary prospect given that, at the time, midway through 2020, a high percentage of people who went to ventilation units were not coming out. Thankfully, she recovered enough that she was able to avoid hospitalisation, but it was a challenging time for both of us. I know that I needed to use some of the techniques I've shared with you in this book to help overcome the stress I experienced during this situation.

The pandemic might be one of the most recent examples of extreme change in our world, but it is unlikely to be the last. Rather than dealing with anxiety and stress from such situations after the fact, it is much better to develop our mental resilience to help us cope during periods of rapid change. One of the best ways to do this is to adopt a growth mindset.

A growth mindset: the key to embracing change

Adopting a growth mindset is absolutely essential for staying resilient amid any kind of rapid changes. A growth mindset encourages adaptability, learning and taking a positive approach to any challenge. The growth mindset involves seeing challenges as opportunities for growth rather than as obstacles. This perspective allows us to remain motivated and engaged even when faced with difficult challenges and stresses.

Those with a growth mindset view mistakes and failures as valuable learning experiences. This attitude fosters greater resilience by allowing us to recover far quicker from setbacks and use them as a stepping stone for future improvement and progress.

Rapid changes often require flexibility and the ability to pivot or change as and when needed. A growth mindset encourages experimentation and openness to new ideas, making it easier for us to adjust our strategies and behaviours in response to changing conditions.

When you have a growth mindset, you are also likely to persist in the face of difficulties, rather than giving up, because you believe that effort and dedication can and does lead to improvement and success. This strengthens your capacity to endure and thrive even under the harshest of pressure and conditions. A growth mindset is also associated with optimism and the belief in your ability to develop skills and competencies. This positive outlook can reduce stress, anxiety and many other mental health conditions. As a result, you can focus on actionable solutions rather than feeling overwhelmed by change.

People with a growth mindset actively seek feedback and use it constructively to enhance their performance. This openness helps them to continuously refine their skills and stay relevant in rapidly changing environments. A growth mindset nurtures a culture of curiosity and creativity, which is essential for innovation. By fostering these qualities, a growth mindset provides a robust framework for resilience allowing us to not only survive, but excel amid rapid changes and uncertainties.

Part Three: Creating Lasting Change

Understanding growth and fixed mindsets

The concept of a growth mindset was introduced by psychologist Carol Dweck and has been the subject of extensive research. Dweck identified two mindsets – a growth mindset and a fixed mindset.

An article for *Lepaya* defines a growth mindset as one that sees abilities as malleable, and embraces challenges and feedback for continuous improvement. Employees with a growth mindset often feel far more empowered and committed than those with a fixed mindset.

Meanwhile, the article describes a fixed mindset, sometimes known as a predetermined mindset, as a belief system that suggests our abilities, intelligence and talents are fixed traits. In other words, a person with a fixed mindset believes they are born with a certain amount of skills or intelligence, and that this cannot change significantly over their lifetime.[26]

This means for someone with a fixed mindset, making an effort and trying your best to become better is futile; if you're a real genius, you shouldn't have to strive. If you struggle in a particular area, trying to improve is essentially futile. People with a fixed mindset are often inflexible in their views about talents and abilities, believing them to be fixed. They also tend to avoid challenges because of their fear of failure, are often dismissive of feedback and feel threatened by others' success.

Those with a growth mindset, on the other hand, are motivated to continuously develop their abilities, stretching themselves to learn new skills and embracing the ongoing journey of development. Whilst some of the traits can apply to differing degrees within both mindsets, and

---

26   Lepaya (2023) *Growth mindset – the mindset that stimulates empowerment.* https://www.lepaya.com/blog/101-growth-mindset.

indeed not all those with a generally fixed mindset will have the same characteristics (and the same goes for those of the growth mindset persuasion), this describes the two approaches in general terms. We always have to remember that as humans we are all individuals and no one can be accurately boxed into one type or another.

Why adopt a growth mindset?

Studies have demonstrated various benefits of adopting a growth mindset in different contexts. For example, one study found that students with a growth mindset tend to achieve higher grades and more academic success than those with its opposite, a fixed mindset.[27] Students with a growth mindset are more likely to embrace challenges, persist through great difficulties and view efforts as a path to mastering their skill.

A further 2022 study concluded that a growth mindset refers to our core belief that our talents can be developed through practice, which may influence our thoughts and behaviours.[28] In this study, the researchers asked over 2,500 first-year students at a university in China to self-assess their mental health. They discovered that the students within the growth mindset group scored significantly lower on "mental health issues" and "stress due to life events" than the students in the fixed mindset group.

This suggests that individuals with a growth mindset are less prone to mental health problems than individuals with a fixed mindset.

---

27 *Changing students' mindsets about learning improves grades* (August 2019). https://news.stanford.edu/stories/2019/08/changing-students-mindsets-learning-improves-grades.

28 Tao, W. *et al.* (2022) 'The influence of growth mindset on the mental health and life events of college students.' *Frontiers in Psychology*, 13. https://doi.org/10.3389/fpsyg.2022.821206.

They view setbacks as opportunities to learn and improve rather than indicators of fixed ability, which helps them to recover and continue striving towards their goals.

Meanwhile, another study published in Research Gate in 2023, demonstrated that students with a growth mindset showed higher levels of motivation and engagement, resilience, academic performance and were more likely to set learning goals, show interest in their studies and take on challenging tasks.[29]

A growth mindset isn't only beneficial when we're studying though. Another piece of research found that employees with a growth mindset tend to have higher life and job satisfaction than those with a fixed mindset.[30] A growth mindset fosters continuous learning and adaptability, which is crucial for career advancement and satisfaction.

Having a growth mindset also helps us to manage mental and emotional stress and anxiety. A study published in EdCentral reported on the negative impact of students with a fixed mindset versus students with a growth mindset.[31]

Jessica Schleider and John Weisz also tested whether a growth mindset intervention could mean adolescents with intense symptoms of anxiety and depression were able to improve their ability to cope with stress and reduce anxiety and depression.

---

29   Jaidumrong, Nutchanat & Mahapoonyanont, Natcha & Songsang, Nuttapong & Gudmundsson, Magnus. (2023). Effect of growth mindset on the academic achievement of students.

30   Kondratowicz B, Dorota Godlewska- W. Growth mindset and life and job satisfaction: the mediatory role of stress and self-efficacy. Health Psychol Rep. 2022 Oct 5;11(2):98-107. doi: 10.5114/hpr/152158. PMID: 38084317; PMCID: PMC10670786.

31   Busch, B. (2018) *Could growth mindset support students' mental health, as well as their learning?* https://edcentral.uk/edblog/expert-insight/growth-mindset-students-mental-health-learning.

Their work suggested that young people who developed a growth mindset fared considerably better than those who did not. In the short term, having a growth mindset also boosted physiological recovery following a socially stressful task.[32]

Interestingly, when they revisited the young people involved in the study nine months later, those who received the growth mindset intervention showed significant improvements for their depression, as well as encouraging results for anxiety.[33]

This again underlines the brain-body – or what I like to call the mindset-body – connection. Our mindset powers the brain, thoughts, feelings and, of course, also directly impacts the physical and physiological. I think the more we recognise and see our brain as another body part, the more we can harness its great potential as well as manage and guide it as we would want.

I'm particularly interested in growth mindsets and know firsthand from 20+ years of seeing many different people with many different issues, how our brain, thoughts, habits, patterns and feelings can all change. As I explained earlier, our brains are "neuroplastic" and can change. However, wanting that change and recognising that change is needed, or at least would be beneficial, is required for our brains to change.

Without this desire to change, it's too easy to stay where we are. That's why many of us get "stuck in our ways" and as a result

---

[32] Jessica L. Schleider, John R. Weisz, 'Reducing risk for anxiety and depression in adolescents: Effects of a single-session intervention teaching that personality can change', *Behaviour Research and Therapy*, Volume 87, 2016, Pages 170-181, ISSN 0005-7967, https://doi.org/10.1016/j.brat.2016.09.011.

[33] Schleider, J. and Weisz, J. (2017) 'A single-session growth mindset intervention for adolescent anxiety and depression: 9-month outcomes of a randomized trial,' *Journal of Child Psychology and Psychiatry*, 59(2), pp. 160–170. https://doi.org/10.1111/jcpp.12811.

become stuck in our own way, by blocking or stopping that crucial mindset shift and mind transformation. We are indeed all creatures of habit, but I hope this book has shown you how we can change and change very much for the better.

Manifestation and the growth mindset is something I'm passionate about, hence why I have recorded many manifestation and law of attraction-style hypnotherapy audio sessions for my app, *Subconsciously*. When we have a purpose, a positive goal and a direction of travel, we are much more likely to pursue unlimited success – whatever success looks like for you.

The role of self-belief in the growth mindset

Self-belief plays a crucial role in the growth mindset, and is also a major area of my clinical hypnotherapy work. Much of my daily work is helping build up my clients' self-belief, self-confidence and self-love through repeated hypnotic suggestions, visualisation, affirmations and anchors.

In the 20th century psychologists began empirically testing and broadening our knowledge on self-belief and the growth mindset. Two of the most influential modern theories are Carol Dweck's research on growth mindset and Albert Bandura's self-efficacy theory. In her article "Rediscovering the power of self belief" Belynder Walia explains how these theories deepen our understanding of how self-belief shapes behaviour, motivation and success across various domains of life, offering empirical frameworks for ideas that align with early philosophical perspectives on the active role of the self.[34]

---

34 Walia B. *Rediscovering the power of self-belief* (2024). https://www.bps.org.uk/psychologist/rediscovering-power-self-belief.

Albert Bandura's self-efficacy theory provides a foundational understanding of how belief in one's abilities influences motivation, behaviour and success. Self-efficacy discusses an individual's belief in their capacity to perform tasks and achieve specific goals. Bandura (1977) demonstrated that self-efficacy is a crucial determinant of how people think, feel and act. People with high self-efficacy approach complex tasks as challenges to be mastered, persist through obstacles and achieve success. In contrast, those with low self-efficacy tend to avoid difficulties, give up easily and limit their personal growth opportunities.

In this way, these terms relate also to the fixed or growth mindset we discussed earlier. These core areas of self-efficacy, self-belief and growth versus fixed mindset delve into the majority of hypnotherapy work. Whether I am helping chronic anxiety sufferers, agoraphobics, sugar addicts, smokers, functioning alcoholics (and/or borderline alcoholics) the list goes on, hypnotherapy helps to rewire and program a new self-efficacy, self-mastery and more positive use of our incredible brain.

Bandura also introduced the concept of social modelling, emphasising the importance of observing others. Seeing others successfully navigate challenges can reinforce one's own belief in their abilities. This phenomenon plays a crucial role in educational and professional settings, as observing peers or colleagues when they excel can boost an individual's sense of self-belief.

Carol Dweck's research on mindsets builds on the concept of self-belief by examining how beliefs about learning and ability influence motivation. According to Dweck, those with a growth mindset are more likely to embrace challenges, persist through challenges and view effort as essential to attain mastery.

Neuroscientific research supports Dweck's findings. Moser et al. (2011) demonstrated that individuals with a growth mindset exhibit more remarkable neural plasticity – the brain's ability to adapt to new information as we have touched on earlier. People with a growth mindset demonstrated more significant brain activity in the anterior cingulate cortex, which is associated with adaptive post-error adjustments.[35] This suggests that self-belief is not only a psychological factor, but also tied to the brain's capacity for growth and resilience.

Harnessing feedback through a growth mindset

I have a growth mindset myself and whenever I see a setback, I use my hypnosis skills to take the emotion out of the situation and refocus my energy to where it is best placed. When it comes to all areas of my life, I am always looking for ways to improve. As such I seek out opportunities to create feedback loops that can help me to learn and see situations from new perspectives. In doing so, I am able to turn setbacks into positives and use these as springboards for success, strength and rewards.

Without constructive feedback it can be difficult to gauge progress and identify areas for improvement. The solution here is to seek feedback from peers, mentors and coaches, as well as to be open to criticism. When you are able to do this, you can use constructive feedback to guide your development. The keys are to practise active listening and apply feedback to foster growth by focusing on the learning process and skills you're developing.

---

35   Moser, J.S. *et al.* (2011) 'Mind your errors,' *Psychological Science*, 22(12), pp. 1484–1489. https://doi.org/10.1177/0956797611419520.

Acknowledge the small steps of progress you make along the way and view each of these as part of a larger journey. You have to create a culture that values learning over performance, which can be a challenge in and of itself. I've found the best way to do this is to surround yourself with like-minded individuals who support your growth efforts and provide encouragement in your pursuit of personal and professional development.

Barry's story: setting up a new life

Barry came to see me for a boost in confidence before moving his whole life and business to a new country. He was planning to uproot his plumbing business and take it from the UK to Spain. He didn't speak Spanish and he knew nobody there, but he had made a decision to take the plunge.

He came to see me for hypnosis to help remove any anxiety he was feeling about making such a huge change. He also wanted to affirm his decision and replace his anxiety with positive confidence.

Session by session, we built up his confidence and reinforced the fact that this was the right decision for him, his family, his business and his life. After four sessions, he knew he could make the transition work for him, his daughter and his wife. Our sessions gave him a powerful boost. It gives me great pleasure to hear from him and see how much he is enjoying his new life in Spain, integrating with the local community and building a thriving business there.

Barry's openness to hypnosis and his positive approach helped ensure this would work for him and it's brilliant to see how he's embraced this change and grasped success with both hands.

Challenges to adopting a growth mindset

Adopting a growth mindset can be really transformative, but it does come with challenges. Often we hold deep-rooted beliefs about intelligence and our abilities being innate and unchangeable, which can make it difficult to embrace a growth mindset. The idea that our intelligence and competencies can't change or evolve is a sign of fixed mindset beliefs.

The solution to this challenge is to recognise and question those beliefs. Instead of telling yourself that you can't do something, focus on finding examples of individuals who have succeeded through effort and perseverance. Practice self-reflection to identify these fixed mindset thoughts and reframe them into new, growth mindset-focused beliefs.

The fear of making mistakes can also prevent us from taking risks and trying new things, which can hold us in a fixed mindset. To overcome this, we need to embrace failure as a learning opportunity, analyse our mistakes to understand what went wrong and use the knowledge we gain from doing so to improve. Once we do so, it's vital to celebrate our effort and progress rather than just the outcomes we achieve.

Another challenge that can hold us back from embracing a growth mindset is comfort and routine. This can discourage the pursuit of new challenges. When we get too used to being in our comfort zone, it becomes harder to break free of it and push the boundaries of what's possible.

One way to challenge this is by setting specific and achievable goals to push your boundaries. You can then gradually increase the level of difficulty and complexity of the goals you're striving for to build your confidence and competence over time. Listening to hypnosis exercises and writing down affirmations in your journal on a daily basis can further help you cement a new mindset and a new habit pattern. This can quiet any internal criticism and doubt that can undermine your efforts to cultivate a growth mindset.

Instead you have to find a way to replace negative self-talk with positive affirmations and remind yourself of past successes. Keeping a journal of progress, which includes lots of positive experiences, will help to reinforce growth-orientated thinking.

> **Time out: affirmations for a growth mindset**
>
> Close your eyes and press your thumb and middle finger together. Take two deep, slow breaths, breathing in through your nose and out through your mouth. Next repeat the following affirmations two to three times to yourself:
>
> → I nurture my own growth mindset.
> → I can be and do.
> → I embrace challenges.
> → I create solutions.
> → I make things happen successfully.
> → I embrace a powerful growth mindset consistently.
> → I turn any setbacks into learning as part of my powerful growth mindset.
>
> Once you have repeated those affirmations as many times as you need, open your eyes and continue reading.

Change is inevitable

Change is an inevitable part of life and growth. By embracing it with an open, positive, flexible and confident mindset, we can unlock opportunities for great personal development, resilience and new possibilities in life. This is the type of hypnotic suggestion that I weave into many of my sessions with clients to create a platform for new beginnings or enhancing and increasing successes. In doing so, I facilitate positive transformations in many people's lives.

While change can be uncomfortable and uncertain, learning to adapt to it allows us to not only survive, but thrive, in evolving circumstances and an ever-changing and very fast-paced world. Instead of fearing the unknown, approaching change with curiosity and a willingness to learn also helps us to navigate transitions more smoothly. We can then come out the other side as stronger, healthier, happier, calmer, more successful, more fulfilled individuals.

> **Time out: accepting and harnessing change**
>
> Let your eyes close. Take a nice couple of deep breaths, inhaling relaxation and exhaling tension. Imagine a balloon underneath your belly button. As you inhale, imagine white particles of relaxing energy swirling around as the balloon inflates and your stomach rises. As the balloon deflates, and your stomach and chest fall, you exhale tension.
>
> Now press together your thumb and middle finger or your thumb and index finger and repeat the following affirmations:
>
> → I embrace change with balance, confidence and an inner calm.
> → I embrace change with a positive focus and it creates a new peace of mind within me.
>
> Once you've repeated those affirmations a few times, take another deep breath and open your eyes.

Remember that embracing change is one of the keys to unlocking a more fulfilling, more stimulating, more rewarding and more wonderful life. Accepting and embracing change will also increase levels of emotional, physical and mental wellbeing, and lead to better health, both now and for the long term. Embracing change also increases resilience.

So, answer the call to embrace change positively, confidently and fearlessly.

Chapter Nine

The Transformative Power of Hypnotherapy

As you will know by now, hypnosis is the instrument that I put a lot of faith and credit in. In the years that I've been practising hypnotherapy and hypnosis, I have seen countless clients transform their lives through these practices. Even if they start out cynical and sceptical, they have enough belief in the process to at least try hypnotherapy and put their faith in me, which I always find humbling. I'm always appreciative of the power of the work I do, and the power of hypnosis and its capacity for rewiring and reprogramming new thought patterns.

Before we end our journey together, I'd like to share a few more of my clients' stories to further cement just how transformative hypnotherapy can be.

Tony's story: overcoming crippling fear

Tony is an A-list celebrity who wanted sessions with me. He had such crippling anxiety that we had to do our sessions via video, because he couldn't leave his house. When we started our sessions, he hadn't left his house for two months because doing so gave him panic attacks. He had become so fearful of these panic attacks that he had developed agoraphobia.

This was not only affecting him on a personal level. It was also preventing him from working as he was unable to leave the house to shoot a new film he was starring in. His fear was crippling, debilitating and it was ruining his life.

As I do with all of my clients, session by session we set out to reprogram his subconscious, with the intention of making him feel confident and comfortable about being on his own and leaving his home. We really focused on positive feelings and confidence around returning to a film set. He loved acting and his desire to return to it drove him to find a way to overcome his fear.

It was a privilege to see his return to confidence. I watched as he learnt to manage his adrenaline, cortisol levels and anxiety. Step by step, quite literally, he was able to get out of the house. Eventually, after about five sessions, he got into the car to drive to the film studios. He was able to get back to his passion – acting – without falling into the cycle of fear that had trapped him for two months.

Through hypnotherapy, we replaced his fear with confidence and an expectation of enjoyment. This allowed him to control his anxiety, restoring balance in his life.

Estelle's story: from insomnia to deep sleep

Estelle was one of those lucky people who could always sleep a good eight hours without waking up. Before she had a child, sleep was her superpower. Even in the first couple of years with a baby, she was still able to sleep. However, one night when her child was around three years old, she started to worry – what if I don't sleep at all? What if I'm not able to function tomorrow? How will I cope at work? How will I deal with my toddler if I haven't slept?

This negative thought loop went round and round in her head. She couldn't sleep a wink. This was a turning point. Estelle went from having several hours of good-quality sleep every night to not being able to sleep at all.

In the following weeks she tried everything – sleeping drugs, valium, even tetrahydrocannabinol (THC). Nothing helped. The THC actually created paranoia and even more anxiety. This was when she came to me for hypnotherapy. Session by session we reprogrammed and rewired her brain so that she no longer had a fear of not being able to sleep, and gave her an expectation of enjoying sleep and sleeping well, just as she had before having a child.

The hypnosis helped her let go of the fear cycle and created a calm confidence that she could sleep when needed and would feel good the next day. There was no pressure, anxiety or stress about going to bed. Our sessions had the desired effect and Estelle returned to a consistent, positive and enjoyable sleep pattern, where she woke up feeling well-rested and ready for the day.

Jill's story: fighting an irrational fear

Jill's story is one that I found particularly fascinating. She had developed obsessive compulsive disorder (OCD) which in her case had manifested out of the blue due to a fear of what happens when you die.

Initially, Jill tried to solve this herself by developing a mindset of being religious. The problem was, Jill wasn't religious by nature, and she swung between believing in an afterlife and being an atheist, believing that after death there is nothing. Both states were causing her anxiety and fear. On the one hand she might be punished by the deity she worshipped and sent to Hell. On the other hand, there was no afterlife to strive for.

Switching between being religious and being an atheist was creating more and more anxiety, compulsions, and repetitive and intrusive thoughts. She oscillated between being religious and being an atheist every few days, stuck in a vicious cycle that always seemed to lead to panic attacks.

At just 23 years old, she had her whole life ahead of her. It was clear that she needed to make some changes to ensure she could live and enjoy her life. Through hypnotherapy, we reset her rationality, positive expectation and we clarified and rebalanced her beliefs around what happens when you die. Our aim was to create a sense of peace for her, so that she would no longer fixate on what might happen after death.

The results were significant and fast – after just one session Jill's mind started to change. Through hypnotic suggestions that I instilled in her subconscious mind, she was able to nullify her old habit patterns that led to fear and panic, and instead could create a new, positive energy. We focused on bringing her back to a place of balance, where she felt in control of her own mind once again.

It wasn't only Jill who was grateful for the transformation. I remember her dad even phoned me to thank me for helping his daughter to overcome the crippling OCD that had been ruining her life.

OCD in its most extreme forms can cause extremely distressing unwanted thoughts, creating a powerful anxiety loop that it is difficult to break free of alone. I've found hypnosis is particularly effective for treating OCD because it reprograms and rewires the brain so that it gravitates towards a new solution and way of thinking entirely. This is often much more effective than other methods that give you tools to help you avoid thinking about the problem, without providing an alternative way of thinking for the long term.

Peter's story: from addiction to clarity

Peter came to see me to get help with his Tramadol addiction. The irony is that he only became addicted to this prescription drug after a friend suggested it might help him take the edge off his stress and help him focus more.

As the owner of three businesses this sounded great, so Peter gave Tramadol a try and within a couple of months had become psychologically dependent on it. He felt it gave him a clearer mind and said that it helped him feel calmer and happier when he was faced with stressful situations at work. As a result, he had been increasing his dosage and had built up a tolerance to the drug. This meant he was taking unhealthy levels of Tramadol on a daily basis.

It took us six sessions of hypnosis to get him completely off Tramadol. Each week we cut down the amount he was taking. By the fifth session, he was off the drug completely and we were merely reinforcing the benefits he felt from not taking Tramadol.

Despite Peter's earlier belief, what he realised during our sessions was that he was happier, more productive, more confident and more peaceful when he wasn't taking Tramadol. He noticed that he felt better physically, mentally, emotionally and spiritually without the drug. All of this helped him to break his largely psychological addiction to Tramadol.

Prakash's story: last chance saloon

When Prakash came to my practice he was desperate to find a way to save his marriage, which was hanging by a thread. Prakash had become addicted to alcohol and every now and then he also mixed this with cocaine.

He was stuck in a cycle of just about making it through the day at work, only to go out and get very drunk in the evenings. His wife made it clear to me during that first session that this was his last chance to save their marriage.

I knew that the hypnotherapy needed to work for Prakash if he was to improve his life. Within just one session, he had stopped drinking. Over the course of the five sessions we had together, we reinforced the positive and amazing natural sense of ecstasy that came from being free of drink and drugs.

What's remarkable is that it has now been 15 years since our sessions and not only is Prakash still sober, but he completely rebuilt his relationship with his wife and they are now very happy and have two children together.

His was a particularly dramatic change in behaviour that demonstrated to me how quickly hypnotherapy can rewire your mindset. Prakash's desire to quit drinking and save his marriage no doubt played a part in how effective our first session was. However, his story is one of the cases that reaffirmed my belief in the power of this process for creating positive, sustained change in people's lives.

Greg's story: number crunching

Greg came to me with a fear of maths. He was a bright 40-something business/government consultant. Although he was perfectly able to perform the kind of maths we all need day-to-day, whenever any maths was involved in a work context it would trigger an irrational anxiety attack. His palms would become sweaty and he'd experience the usual adrenaline responses. Greg was the first client I had seen with fear of maths (though not necessarily the last!).

Maths was definitely my worst subject at school, so I sympathised. Session by session the hypnosis worked as I hoped, and a new mindset of no fear and no anxiety around all things maths became the new norm for Greg.

Tony's story: creating better balance

A prominent MP contacted me while I was writing this book to ask for a session. He had previously seen me about an anxiety issue, so he was very open to hypnosis and understood its power for transformation. This time he wanted help to balance work stress as a result of a very heavy workload and significant demands on his time.

Our sessions went very well and we created a mindset establishing a greater sense of balance, and perspective, while de-stressing, rewiring and re-energising. This also helped improve the efficiency of his energy throughout the rigours of what are often 14-hour days.

John's story: teeing up for positive self-talk

A world-class golfer emailed me after missing the cut and playing way below his best golf. I've helped many golfers in the past and recognise it as being one of the most psychological of all sports. With golf, all it takes is a millisecond of negative thought, or any kind of unwanted intrusive thought, and suddenly you've hit the ball many metres off target and it lands somewhere in the middle of a mini forest, or worse still straight into a lake.

John spent some time in our first session explaining how when he plays with other top golfers such as Rory McIlroy or Scottie Scheffler, he hits the ball just as well as them, and knows the only difference is what is between their ears. John will be impacted by negative thoughts and self-doubt, thoughts like, "You're going to mess this up", and "Look how many spectators there are today, don't f**k this up" creep into his internal narrative.

By contrast, his peers who have won more titles and have been consistently in the world's top ten, have a consistency of confidence, positive focus, and complete faith and trust in themselves, their abilities and their game. This extends to when they hit bad shots, or are not doing so well.

Drumming in this confidence, creating a positive focus and flipping negative self-talk was what I needed to do with John in our sessions and that's exactly what we did. I'm happy to say John's results picked up significantly. After seeing me, he was playing in what I call "the ultimate confidence zone" with "a solid impenetrable armour" around him. His position on the world rankings climbed higher and higher and he was finishing competitions placed much higher up. The relief I saw in his whole body language each session was wonderful to see.

Declan's story: overcoming a fear of relationships

Obsessive compulsive disorder (OCD) involves anxiety and a great deal of stress. The sufferer feels the need to compulsively overthink about specific issues. This can extend to virtually any trigger and is not limited to stereotypical examples such as germs and hand cleaning, or whether the tap or light was turned off.

Declan came to me because of his OCD around fear of intimacy and relationships. In his case, there was also a degree of limerence, which refers to a state of mind that results from romantic feelings, typically involving intrusive and melancholic thoughts. Declan had undergone years of counselling with limited success, at times he had become suicidal.

He knew rationally that his responses were completely irrational, but he couldn't change them. If he sensed a woman liked him or felt any kind of emotional feelings towards him, it would trigger a panic attack and a set of extreme overthinking and overanalysing.

He would always need to end whatever kind of relationship they had. Most of these relationships were non-intimate and non-consumate because he feared anything becoming more serious. When he came to me, a beautiful woman at work had shown some interest in him, and they had slept together when he was extremely drunk. They both agreed it was a one-off thing.

Over the following weeks he had a multitude of intrusive thoughts about her and whether she liked him, whether he liked her and even loved her, or whether she may even love him. His anxiety would run ragged. It was non-stop and this over-questioning became never ending.

This type of pattern had been going on for multiple years, which meant Declan had never been able to have a relationship, although he was happy on his own. Our sessions focused on managing the anxiety, letting go of worry about whether the woman at work (or any other woman) showed a liking for him and whether he may like her back. I focused on creating hypnotic suggestions around feeling entirely comfortable whether a woman showed any kind of real, potential or imagined interest in him. The sessions had the required impact of creating positive control over his mind and mindset. This gave Declan a sense of peace from all the overthinking.

Whilst it was limerence of a kind, this case involved a complex interweaving of emotions and an uncertainty and fear around romantic feelings and whether indeed Declan was even feeling them. You may wonder whether this stemmed from his childhood – had Declan's mother been unable to provide him with intimacy? Did his father run off with another woman, leaving his mother alone and distraught? (You get the picture). But the answer is no. He had an entirely normal upbringing in a close-knit family.

In many cases I find there is no clear event or events in childhood that cause the issues my clients face. This is one of the reasons why I prefer to focus on the present, than to delve into the past.

Mark's story: learning to move on

Mark was experiencing a clear degree of limerence when he came to see me. He wanted help to get over his ex. He had dumped her about two years previously, but had regretted it in the weeks and months that followed. This culminated in him not being able to get her out of his mind, creating a state of severe anxiety and overthinking around what could have been.

He was an old school romantic and he told me he was worried that he may have let "the one" go. This thought was troubling him day and night, a full three years post separation. She had moved on and it was clear she was very happy with her partner. Intrusive images, jealous thoughts, unrequited love and the discomfort of not knowing what might have been were amongst the core issues we needed to fix with the hypnotherapy.

This type of issue usually requires more sessions than others. I believe this is due to the slightly different and more complex emotions involved with relationships and the psychological impacts post-relationship. We focused on this session by session.

Mark grew better able to distance himself from the intrusive thoughts and better able to flip negative into positive mindset thinking. He told himself that he would find the right woman for him, that his ex wasn't the right one and their relationship ended for a reason. I built in confidence that he would move on stronger, wiser and better. I saw Mark consistently progress and a positive energy rose within him session by session.

Heather's story: burned by love

Heather came to see me after a married man she was having an affair with had ended their relationship. She found him highly charismatic, and he was in a powerful and influential position within the same line of business as her.

She told me she believed he was narcissistic, but she was overthinking, overanalysing and causing herself great distress as the ending seemed to her to have come during a wonderful part of their relationship. We needed to focus on regaining her strength, her power, her balance and her control. The hypnotic suggestions did just that. Session by session, Heather regained her sense of self, her confidence, her power and was able to move on and heal faster.

About a year and a half later, Heather contacted me to request further sessions. After about a year, the charismatic man had talked her back into a relationship, only to once again dump her a few months later.

She knew how well the hypnosis had worked previously and had full trust in me and the process (an important part of successful outcomes for hypnotherapy). She was possibly even more distressed this time, so in these sessions we focused on managing overthinking and helping her to regain not only control, but also the strength, to not let herself be taken in and then let go of in a repeated cycle in future. The sessions helped relieve the anxiety of her overthinking turmoil. So far as I know she hasn't let him back again (but watch this space).

Sheri's story: developing a healthy relationship with food

Binge eating is a very common issue I help with. It's a well-known disorder that causes a lot of distress to sufferers, including anxiety and depression, along with the physical ill effects of obesity and excessive sugar consumption, which is often what binge eaters choose as their food to binge on.

That said, binge eaters can and do binge on any food. They do so completely irrespective of whether they are physiologically hungry. This condition is centred around psychology which then feeds (no pun intended) into the food they eat. Whether when bored, for comfort, due to stress, when alone, or for absolutely no reason, the unhealthy bingeing cycle occurs.

Sheri came to me really needing to manage her eating habits and treat the disorder. Session by session, a new healthier pattern was being established. The hypnotic suggestions were focused around her seeing food as fuel, and severing links to using food like a drug (an emotional chemical tool). The aim was for her to enjoy it around the normal mealtimes in the day and to see food as enjoyable, but also as a source of nutrients, which deliver health and are life sustaining.

I built Sheri's confidence that she could and would create this healthy relationship with food long term. After our sessions she explained that the hypnotherapy had a "100 per cent positive impact". She felt no need for snacks and enjoyed a lighter, satisfying feeling in her stomach after eating, rather than the bloated, over-full, uncomfortable feelings she experienced in the past.

Like all psychological issues, binge eating is not gender specific and I've seen many men as well as women who need help with this disorder.

An A-lister's story: up in smoke

About two years ago, an A-list celebrity couple contacted me because they both wanted to stop vaping. This is an issue I help many people with since vaping has taken off in the past five years. I saw the couple separately, starting with the wife, whose session went really well.

Then the husband came for his hypnotherapy. He told me he was surprised I hadn't dangled a watch in front of him and I explained that the days of hypnotising people using a watch on a pendulum were long gone. All I needed were my voice and my words. Our session also progressed smoothly. A month later, they contacted me to say that their vape addiction had gone.

They were very pleased with the outcome and they have even referred friends – both from showbiz and not – to me since.

Andrea's story: opening up to intimacy

Andrea came to see me because she was suffering from vaginismus. She was in her 30s and had never been able to have intercourse. Vaginismus is a psychological condition, where a fear of pain during intercourse creates a muscle reaction that closes the vaginal opening. She had been to various "specialists", tried botox and even had surgery. However, these physical interventions had not worked because the core psychological trigger had not been treated.

The hypnotic suggestions I used focus on relaxation of mind, an expectation of pleasure not pain, and feeling comfortable about opening to allow in. The sessions worked faster than with other vaginismus clients I had seen. Within just two sessions, Andrea was able to insert dilators in her vagina for the first time. After a couple more sessions, she was able to enjoy intercourse with her partner for the first time.

I will always remember her wonder at how years of therapy and interventions had failed to help her, yet within just a handful of hypnotherapy sessions she was able to fully overcome vaginismus.

Stevie's story: addicted to viagra

My first TV appearance was on a BBC program about a man dependent on viagra. Stevie turned up along with TV presenter Cherry Healey. They set up in my office and we began filming. I did what I normally do, speaking to him about the issue of performance anxiety. In no time, it felt as though the camera wasn't there.

The suggestions I used focused around him feeling confident about easily and effortlessly gaining and sustaining an erection, and enjoying being fully in the moment during sex. The result was great for him and his beaming smile on our follow up session told its own story. The hypnotherapy had worked a treat.

Sue's story: reaching new levels

Channel 5 were doing a session involving Sue, who had a fear of lifts. She had to walk up multiple stairs at her workplace, not to mention endure various other inconveniences as a result of this phobia. Again the film crew set up and I set about my business as though the cameras weren't even there. The hypnosis worked very well.

Immediately after her session we used the lift in my office building to go up four floors. Sue was able to do it confidently and the joy on her face as she stepped out on the fourth floor was wonderful. I remember giving her a big hug. She let me know in a text a few days later that she had gone up the elevator in the Shard in London to the 52nd floor bar to celebrate her 60th birthday. I think her fear of lifts is gone for good.

Dr Tulleken's story: an unusual request

Channel 4 wanted to do a program involving TV presenter Dr Tulleken, whose goal was to be hypnotised to be comfortable eating insects to showcase the powers of hypnosis. He had previously felt disgusted at the thought of putting the likes of grasshoppers and mealworms in his mouth.

The film crew again set up and I set about my work with the insects – grasshoppers, crickets and mealworms – on my table ready to be consumed after the session (if the session worked). The session worked very well and before long Dr Tulleken was munching down grasshoppers like there was no tomorrow. I joined in too, to show I wasn't perturbed. They tasted of very little, and they definitely could have used some oil and seasoning (next time perhaps).

Linda's story: escaping an escalating fear

Writer Linda Grant came to see me many years back with a fear of escalators. She had suddenly frozen with fear when attempting to head down the Oxford Circus escalator. She couldn't believe it, as it had come out of nowhere. We focused the session on the hypnotic suggestion and visuals around her feeling entirely comfortable and confident walking up to the escalator and heading down it.

We also worked on her having no issues going down or up any length of escalator. As is often the case for my other former escalator phobics, the longer escalators tend to cause more panic and anxiety. The sessions went well. About two weeks later I saw just how well, with an article in *The Guardian* newspaper documenting her successful trial of hypnotherapy.

Melanie's story: overcoming stage fright

Melanie came to see me with a severe public speaking phobia, which had arisen when her leg had started shaking during a session. She had to present to the CEO of Apple and all the other Apple big wigs at the company's annual conference, and she was terrified.

We focused on her feeling able to comfortably, easily and confidently channel and use adrenaline and nervous energy during her upcoming presentation. The aim was for her to feel not only comfortable about adrenaline, but happy to have and use it for a better performance with greater focus and clarity of mind.

We focused on the positive control of adrenaline (where it would not control her at all). I asked her to message me after her speech to let me know how it went. She did, and reported there was no leg shaking and that the speech went really well. She received excellent feedback from colleagues. Public speaking anxiety is one of the most common issues I help with. Hypnotherapy works so well to help people overcome this anxiety, as it does with so many other types of performance-related anxieties.

Natalie's story: mastering the mind-body connection

Natalie came to me for help with her IBS – irritable bowel syndrome is a gastrointestinal disorder characterised by symptoms of abdominal pain. These symptoms are always worsened by an increase of stress and anxiety. Natalie's IBS would flare up badly whenever she would travel by train or plane, or when she went somewhere like the cinema where she would feel trapped and unable to easily reach a toilet should she need one in a "bowel emergency".

This worry would trigger an IBS flare up. It also further emphasises the powerful connection between our guts and our brain. In the past Natalie, and most other IBS sufferers I've treated, would go to the toilet before almost any event, meeting, or change of situation and setting (even if nothing was there to come out! I sorry I hope you're not reading this whilst eating).

This behaviour becomes a ritual for sufferers to attempt to clear or check their bowels are fully clear (even though they know 95 per cent of their visits will result in nothing being excreted). The inconvenience of IBS is extensive. Many sufferers will stop taking the easy travel route because of a fear of having an episode on a train, bus or plane and instead have to take long detours, often choosing to cycle or walk rather than be trapped on public transport.

Many will avoid social situations such as meeting friends at restaurants because of their preoccupation and anxiety around their IBS, needing the toilet and not wanting to experience panic or anxiety amongst friends and in public.

With Natalie we focused on hypnosis and I used my usual combination of hypnotic suggestion, visualisation, anchors and affirmations. They worked a treat. She felt able to sit in a cinema and near the centre of a row (something she would have never contemplated previously) and watch a film that was a little over three hours long, with no thoughts of needing to go to the toilet. Her subconscious had effectively been rewired and reset to feel calm, comfortable and fully confident that there was no need to worry about having an accident, that her body would always hold on easily and comfortably, and let her know in good time when she actually needed to poo.

Many doctors have referred IBS patients to me, as there is no real medication for this condition and it is directly impacted by psychological triggers and mindset. As a result, I've noticed more and more doctors and people from the medical profession are referring clients to my practice for hypnotherapy.

Hypnotherapy for treating pain

There are a handful of medically unexplained or unexplainable symptoms, and many of these conditions involve some degree of pain. This varies from moderate and lingering to downright horrific pain. The conditions might affect the brain with extreme headaches or dull aches that can often feel as though they are deep within the body's cells. I've seen many such cases where even the most experienced specialist consultants cannot explain or treat the condition.

Many clients tell me they have given up and simply accept the diagnosis that "It's in your head." Though that may seem a little overly direct there is often truth within those statements in the sense that stressing about pain, linger tinnitus (the ringing or buzzing heard from the inner and not caused by an outside source), hot and cold sensations, or other symptoms that the doctors simply cannot diagnose or treat, causes additional heightening of these symptoms. It is a very vicious cycle.

It is well known that stress and anxiety increase cortisol levels. Cortisol, also known as the "stress hormone", is the hormone our bodies release to help us respond to stress and regulate our blood sugar and blood pressure. Increased stress increases blood pressure, creates mood swings, triggers weight gain and much more besides. Anxiety and stress also directly impact our immune system, suppressing its ability to fight infections, increasing the risks of various diseases, delaying the healing of wounds, as well as causing inflammation of the brain and many other things (I think you get the point).

Hypnotherapy helps to manage pain and discomfort, by refocusing attention away from such things as pain or buzzing in the ears and in doing so helps to relax the mind and body. By doing this it helps directly with the body's healing. Destressing is known to improve wound healing and even nerve ending damage. This just goes to show how interconnected our brain and body are.

Tina's story: overcoming extreme pain

Tina first came to see me for help to stop smoking. At the time she had a 40-a-day habit, and after one 50 minute hypnosis session, she kicked it. Her family, and even she herself, were shocked that she could give up a habit she'd held for 30 years, so quickly.

However, when she next came to see me it was for a very different reason. She had collapsed at the gym and been unable to stand or sit for some time. It later transpired she had ruptured her occipital nerve (a nerve between the bone of the spine in the upper neck that spreads through the muscles around the back of the head and scalp). She also had a case of vertigo that had gone undiagnosed by a couple of doctors, which worsened to include severe migraines, tinnitus and chronic lightheadedness.

By the time she came back to me, she had seen multiple doctors, medical specialists, acupuncturists and chiropractors, all to no avail. The conditions she now had were literally ruining her life. As an active older woman she was not used to being unable to do the things she used to do. This was when she got in touch with me.

Session by session, her anxiety and focus on the ringing in her ears reduced. Her migraines became more bearable and less frequent. It was a relief to be on the mend. Whilst hypnosis and hypnotherapy cannot directly mend a damaged nerve ending, by helping with pain management through hypnotic suggestion and mentally dialling down the pain I was able to help her live a better life. I used hypnotic suggestion and visualisation of a pain dial that you control through your mind.

By increasing positivity and confidence that her body would heal, I wouldn't be surprised if Tina's nerve healed more quickly than it would otherwise have done had she not had hypnotherapy sessions. This is because the body heals faster when it is calmer and under less stress, all of which I was able to deliver for Tina.

Cameron's story: healing the body through the mind

Cameron had been hiking in the idyllic scenery of Montana, US. When he returned to the UK about a month later, he felt strange pains and dull aches he had never felt before in his leg. This was confirmed as Lyme disease – a bacterial infection caught from the bite of an infected tick. It's likely Cameron caught it on his hiking expedition.

Lyme's disease can be effectively eliminated with antibiotics and the sooner it's caught, the better. However, Cameron had left it quite a long time (around two months), which meant that the disease was likely to stay with him for at least three months, according to his doctor.

Some nine months later, Cameron was still reporting the pain and dull ache. In our sessions we focused on what we could control and use to better help the body eliminate the disease fully and allow Cameron to return to normality – we used Cameron's mind and mindset. Cameron was anxious about why he was still suffering when his doctors had said the disease should have been cleared months earlier.

Cameron enjoyed our hypnosis sessions, during which I introduced pain management hypnotic suggestions alongside suggestions for unwinding and refocusing his energies with a specific emphasis on positive energy. I wanted Cameron to be confident he would be fully healed. For such diseases and infections that cause damage within the physical body, it is wonderful to hasten the healing process using the mind as a tool.

Its impact on boosting the immune system by destressing and reframing the mindset more positively is something we can all do whenever we choose to. About a month after our sessions, Cameron got the all clear from Lyme disease.

How to find a hypnotherapist

As you've seen through the many examples I've shared in this book, hypnotherapy can be highly effective for treating a range of conditions. If you are considering hypnotherapy as an option, my advice is to seek the support of a qualified, experienced professional who can provide clear and balanced information about how hypnosis works, why it works and how it could help you.

Hypnotherapists such as myself have to be transparent about our processes to help reduce scepticism and show more people the potential this therapy has to transform lives. I encourage you to ask questions, express your concerns and create an open dialogue with any hypnotherapist you are considering working with.

For all that hypnosis can seem like magic – and I have had some clients call me a magician because of the dramatic shifts they've experienced in their lives – the reality is that hypnosis is simply the process by which we can reprogram negative neural pathways and turn them into positive ones.

Anyone can benefit from hypnotherapy. Personally I have found hypnotic suggestion to be especially effective, and many of my clients can attest to its efficacy. This is an uncomplicated, direct and fast way to achieve results. You can use the affirmations I've shared throughout this book to begin to introduce an element of hypnotic suggestion to your own life.

Hypnosis is backed by science and medicine. You are in complete control during your session and the majority of people report that the process is not only enjoyable, but also therapeutic. In fact, hypnotherapy has the same relaxing effect as meditation, but it allows you to go deeper into your subconscious. In doing so, it enables you to overcome challenges in your life in a very quick and positive way.

The power of gratitude

I'd like to share one simple tool that can help transform your life, alongside hypnotherapy or any other kind of therapy you might undergo. That tool is gratitude. This is the starting point for your own happiness.

Without gratitude, we're not open to the great joy in life. We have to recognise that life is incredibly precious. We have an amazing ability to attract positive energy, to energise, to increase and to accumulate, all we have to do is put our focus in the right place.

One of the best tips I can give you is to spend a few minutes each day writing down three things you're grateful for. Doing this will shift your focus from what you're lacking to what you have. This fosters a more positive mindset. A study by Emmons and McCullough in 2003 found that people who regularly wrote down what they were grateful for experienced more positive emotions, felt more alive, slept better, expressed more compassion and kindness and even had stronger immune systems than those who didn't.[36]

Research published in the *Journal of Happiness Studies* also found that gratitude can contribute to a reduction in stress, anxiety and depression.[37]

In short, a gratitude practice helps shift your focus from negative emotions and thoughts to more positive ones. People who practise gratitude tend to report better physical health as well as better mental wellbeing. They even experience longer and better quality sleep, especially if they write in their gratitude journal before bedtime.[38]

Gratitude also plays a significant role in strengthening relationships. Expressing appreciation can lead to increased feelings of connection and satisfaction with our relationships, whether romantic or platonic. It fosters the cycle of positive interactions that strengthens bonds.

---

[36] Emmons, R. A., McCullough, M. E., & Tsang, J.-A. (2003). The assessment of gratitude. In S. J. Lopez & C. R. Snyder (Eds.), *Positive psychological assessment: A handbook of models and measures* (pp. 327–341). American Psychological Association. https://doi.org/10.1037/10612-021

[37] Fekete EM, Deichert NT. A Brief Gratitude Writing Intervention Decreased Stress and Negative Affect During the COVID-19 Pandemic. J Happiness Stud. 2022;23(6):2427-2448. doi: 10.1007/s10902-022-00505-6. Epub 2022 Feb 24. PMID: 35228834; PMCID: PMC8867461.

[38] Wood AM, Joseph S, Lloyd J, Atkins S. Gratitude influences sleep through the mechanism of pre-sleep cognitions. J Psychosom Res. 2009 Jan;66(1):43-8. doi: 10.1016/j.jpsychores.2008.09.002. Epub 2008 Nov 22. PMID: 19073292.

Subconsciously

Research also indicates that gratitude can help individuals become much more resilient, particularly in the face of traumatic events. It helps people recover more effectively from stress and adverse events by promoting a positive outlook on life.[39]

I can vouch for the efficacy of gratitude. It has helped me deal with the extreme stress I've experienced in the years before writing this book. By focusing on gratitude and forgiveness, I have seen a profound positive impact on my life.

This leads perfectly onto where I'd like to leave you in this book – with some final advice for creating a healthier, happier, more fulfilled life for yourself.

---

39   Adams, P.D. (2022) 'Relationships, Resilience, and Wellbeing: The Science of Gratitude | UMGC,' *University of Maryland Global Campus*, 21 November. https://www.umgc.edu/blog/the-science-of-gratitude#4.

Conclusion

Now that you've finished reading, I would love you to take some time to think about how you can use some of the tools and techniques I've shared to achieve lasting happiness in your life. Can you take just five minutes each day to focus on all the positive, rewarding and meaningful things that are happening in your life? Focus on being present and feeling alive.

Use mindfulness techniques, such as focusing on your breathing or the sensations you feel, to ensure you are truly present when you think about these positive aspects of your life. At the same time, appreciate that you don't need to force happiness. Instead, enjoy developing the habit of being more present, and notice how that affects your positivity.

Pause for a moment now and think about how beautiful it is that you're able to read this book. You're taking steps to improve your life, no matter how small. What a wonderful thing to do.

You are capable of more than you realise

We are creatures of habit and it is very easy to get stuck in negative thought loops and patterns of behaviour. But what I hope you've realised from reading this book is that there is potentially more you can achieve in your life. You have the power to live a happier, more positive life. All you have to do is take control of your mind.

When you open your mind to more positivity, the possibilities are endless. You are creating an opportunity to bring greater fulfilment, satisfaction, joy and happiness into your life. You can remove the overcomplication, overthinking and overanalysis. In doing so, you free your mind up to focus on the positive experiences, feelings and sensations that are all around you.

I urge you to be open-minded, proactive and motivated in your pursuit of greater fulfilment. Enjoy every day. Seek out positive change in any situation. Nurture yourself and practice compassion. You are on a journey of self-discovery, as we all are. By reading this book you have taken further positive steps on that journey.

Time out: becoming happier

Let's do a final exercise together. Close your eyes. Press together your thumb and middle finger. Take a couple of nice, deep breaths. Imagine the balloon under your belly. As you inhale, white particles of clear energy fill the balloon and you relax. As you exhale, the balloon deflates and you release tension.

Mentally repeat the following affirmations to yourself:

→ I allow myself to be happy.
→ I prefer to focus on more positive energy in my life.
→ I am here, now, in the moment.
→ I appreciate living.

> Repeat those positive affirmations and words of gratitude to yourself two or three times. Learn them by heart and use them at least twice each day to remind yourself that you deserve to be happy.

Be happy

It sounds like a simple enough instruction. But really take it in. You deserve to be happy. You can allow yourself to be happier. When you are happy, you create happiness for others too. We have a limited time on this planet, and it is much better to spend our time here focusing on the positives than dwelling on the negative.

The beauty of the techniques and affirmations I've shared with you throughout this book is that they are simple to implement in your daily life. You don't need to dedicate hours to these practices. Just a few minutes is enough. Many of them take only seconds to anchor you into a more positive state.

Make a note of the affirmations that have most resonated with you. Learn these and use them whenever you need to. Introduce a gratitude practice and observe how this has a positive impact on every aspect of your life.

As you can see, hypnotherapy is all about harnessing the power of our own minds. By using the tools I've shared with you in this book, you can begin to use hypnotic suggestions to become happier, healthier and more fulfilled.

Final thoughts

Thank you for reading. I have hundreds more interesting case studies to share to showcase the power that lies within us all and our amazing brains, as well as a great deal more interesting science to share about the brain and how neuroscience will look in just a few years from now. I also have plenty more techniques to share with you to help you instantly reset and stop anxiety, boost your confidence, enhance your performance, resist urges to overeat, resist temptations to vape or smoke and much more. But they're for another book. For now, I'll leave you with some final interesting facts about hypnotherapy…

Did You Know?

Top 10 scientifically proven benefits of hypnotherapy

Hypnotherapy is backed by a growing body of scientific and medical research showing its effectiveness in addressing a range of issues. Here are ten scientifically proven benefits of hypnotherapy:

1. **Reduces anxiety and stress:** Studies show that hypnotherapy helps decrease stress and anxiety by relaxing the body and quieting the mind, impacting the autonomic nervous system to reduce physiological stress responses.

2. **Helps manage chronic pain:** Hypnotherapy has been shown to effectively reduce chronic pain, especially in conditions like fibromyalgia, arthritis and migraines. The therapy works by altering how the brain processes pain signals, reducing the perceived intensity.

3. **Supports weight loss:** Hypnosis for weight loss is effective for increasing motivation, changing eating behaviours

and addressing the underlying psychological causes of overeating. Research shows that hypnosis can enhance weight loss efforts when combined with behavioural or cognitive therapies.

4. **Improves sleep quality:** Hypnosis is helpful for insomnia and other sleep disorders, promoting relaxation and reducing racing thoughts. Studies indicate that it can increase the duration of slow-wave sleep, the deep restorative stage of sleep.

5. **Helps quit smoking:** Hypnotherapy has proven effective for smoking cessation, helping break the habit by addressing subconscious triggers and increasing resistance to cravings. Meta-analyses indicate that hypnosis is more effective than other methods for some individuals.

6. **Enhances confidence and self-esteem:** Hypnotherapy can be used to boost self-esteem and confidence by altering limiting beliefs, reducing self-doubt, and reinforcing positive self-image at the subconscious level.

7. **Assists in trauma recovery:** Hypnotherapy is used to treat post-traumatic stress disorder (PTSD) and other trauma-related conditions. By creating a safe mental space, it helps individuals process and reframe traumatic memories without overwhelming emotions.

8. **Reduces symptoms of IBS:** Hypnotherapy is one of the most recommended treatments for IBS, as it helps relax the digestive tract, reduce stress and lessen symptoms like bloating, pain, and discomfort.

9. **Improves focus and concentration:** Hypnosis enhances mental clarity and focus, which can be beneficial in learning,

performance and productivity. Studies indicate that it improves attention span and concentration by quieting distractions and increasing relaxation.

10. **Strengthens emotional regulation:** Hypnotherapy can increase emotional resilience by accessing and reprogramming underlying emotional responses, making it effective for managing anger, grief and other challenging emotions. It has been shown to improve overall emotional health by reshaping automatic reactions.

Top 10 surprising facts about hypnotherapy

Here are ten surprising and lesser-known facts about hypnotherapy that highlight its depth and versatility:

1. **It's been used for thousands of years:** Hypnosis-like practices date back to ancient Egypt, Greece and India. The Greeks, for instance, used "temple sleep", a meditative state believed to help with healing.

2. **It alters brain waves similar to meditation:** Hypnosis shifts the brain into a theta state, similar to meditation and deep relaxation, allowing access to the subconscious. This state can facilitate changes in thought patterns and behaviours.

3. **Can't make you do something against your will:** Contrary to popular myths, hypnotherapy can't make people act against their morals or will. People remain in control throughout the process, and hypnosis merely enhances focus and suggestion responsiveness.

4. **It changes your perception of time:** During hypnotherapy, people often experience time distortion. Sessions might feel

shorter or longer than they are, which can be helpful in cases where intense therapeutic work feels like it went by quickly.

5. **Can be used as anaesthesia:** Hypnosis has been used to reduce or replace anaesthesia for surgery, childbirth, and dental procedures. Known as "hypnoanaesthesia", it has been effective for pain management, especially for patients allergic to conventional anaesthesia.

6. **Effective across cultures and languages:** Studies show that hypnotherapy's effectiveness is universal, as it taps into subconscious processes that transcend cultural differences. The relaxation and suggestion techniques work similarly regardless of language barriers.

7. **Used by top athletes and performers:** Hypnosis is used by elite athletes, musicians and actors to enhance focus, visualise success, reduce performance anxiety and recover from setbacks. Michael Jordan, Tiger Woods and Adele are among those who've used hypnotherapy for peak performance.

8. **Has applications in cancer care:** Hypnotherapy is increasingly recognised for its role in cancer care. It can help manage pain, reduce anxiety and alleviate treatment side effects like nausea, offering patients better overall quality of life.

9. **Can improve immune function:** Research suggests that hypnosis can positively impact the immune system by reducing stress, which is known to impair immune function. Some studies indicate improved antibody response and faster recovery times.

10. **Not everyone is equally hypnotizable:** Studies show that about 10–15 per cent of people are highly hypnotisable,

responding exceptionally well to hypnosis.[40] Hypnotisability varies naturally and can depend on personality traits and openness to suggestion. Perhaps even more surprisingly the level of hypnosis you experience doesn't equate to the results you will see. So in effect, susceptibility to hypnosis doesn't matter.

---

40 *Scientists use high-tech brain stimulation to make people more hypnotizable* (2024). https://med.stanford.edu/news/all-news/2024/01/brain-stimulation-hypnosis.html.

Subconsciously

Subconsciously, your on-the-go hypnotherapist.

Aaron Surtees has transformed lives by rewiring mindsets and breaking mental barriers for over 20 years. His groundbreaking hypnotherapy methods empower world champion athletes, A-list celebrities and high-fliers in the business world.

He has now made his unique methodology available through his hypnotherapy app, *Subconsciously.*

Scan the QR code to download the app, get a free three-day trial and uncover the transformative power of hypnotherapy in your life.

About the Author

Aaron Surtees is the director of City Hypnosis, London's leading hypnotherapy practice. He is trained to the highest level in Advanced Clinical Hypnotherapy and Neuro-Linguistic Programming. He has combined his hypnotic techniques with advanced modern mind programming known as the "Surtees Method".

As a Clinical Hypnotherapist and Psychologist, Aaron has treated many people both in and out of the public eye, including well-known names in sports, music and television. The majority of his clients are high-level professionals based in London, however, Aaron regularly sees clients who travel from around the UK and internationally for sessions with him.

Aaron has appeared on the *BBC*, *Channel 4*, *Channel 5* and in various publications, including *The Daily Mail*, *The Telegraph*,

The Guardian, Cosmopolitan, Forbes, Harper's Bazaar, Business Insider and *The Standard*.

When Aaron isn't using hypnotherapy to help his clients transform their lives, he indulges his keen passion for food and cooking by exploring an eclectic array of restaurants in London. He enjoys cycling, going to the gym, reformer pilates and good wine. He also has a keen interest in listening to music of many genres though mainly, rock, dub, reggae, congolese samba, ambient, dance music and last, but certainly not least, classical music.

Printed in Great Britain
by Amazon